Law Firm Pricing: Strategies, Roles, and Responsibilities

TOBY BROWN AND VINCENT CORDO

Globe Law
and Business

Authors
Toby Brown and Vincent Cordo

Published by
Globe Law and Business Ltd
3 Mylor Close
Horsell
Woking
Surrey GU21 4DD
United Kingdom
Tel: +44 20 3745 4770
www.globelawandbusiness.com

ISBN: 978-1-78358-095-8
ePUBS ISBN: 978-1-78742-747-1
Adobe PDF ISBN: 978-1-78742-748-8

A catalogue record for this book is available from the British Library

Contents

Executive summary

AS LAW firms and their clients evolve in setting ways to predict legal costs – while tracking key metrics/KPIs and producing top tier results – they are investing new thought into pricing and matter management and have begun to hire 'pricing directors' and leaders whose job it is to rationalize, monitor, control, and set strategic pricing.

This report explains the evolution of a finance function within a law firm and the strategic interaction with the client pricing role, explaining the value and benefits this pricing position can provide. It will provide step-by-step guidance for law firm leadership and pricing directors (and their equivalent) as they come to terms with this changing role and its key responsibilities. This report will also be useful for those considering the role of the pricing director and appointing one for their firm.

Much has been written about the changing market for legal services. This report is not more of the same. It is written with the understanding that the reader is already well aware of the market. Clients continue pushing for greater discounts and they want ways to measure quality, and of defining metrics, tools, processes, and value. The industry is pushing for metrics and statistics to help pinpoint the best law firm options to complete a matter and for clients to pick the best firm to fit their needs. Where the technology revolution was once the answer, there is now a glaring need for analysis, a definition of metrics, standards, process setting with expectations to maintain value (defining what value is), and quality, while proving you are being better, faster, and cheaper.

The push for law firms and clients to focus on their pricing and matter management strategies is here. Law firms either need to adapt and embrace these new value approaches and start setting standards, or sit back and watch their bottom lines drop.

This shift in the industry has led many firms and clients to create pricing roles and teams to support this effort. Given the pressures on businesses to keep their spend predictive and for partners to bring in business while maintaining profitability, these roles have quickly become important and have high value to firm leadership as well as amongst clients. The titles for these positions can vary, but generally they evolve into some form of a 'pricing director'. The director level acknowledges the impact on the business of law and the need for high-level skills for the position.

Pricing directors and pricing teams have been thrust into the position of helping their firms and businesses to understand and ultimately adapt to this changing market. This report will explain, in detail, the function of this role, what breadth of skills one needs for it, how the pricing team should be structured, where it sits in an organization, how it interacts with strategy and with clients, and what governance should be set in place to make it work.

More importantly, this is the starting point to the 'how' – how the position works and how to make it truly beneficial to the firm. The position needs to be more than a marketing tag in an RFP response next to the bios; clients want to see testimony in responses without 'cookie cutter' type generic replies to RFPs. From the client's side, they need to have in place a role that knows how to measure metrics while producing results and getting greater control on predictability.

Needless to say, whatever the pricing role starts as, and whichever department it starts in, it invariably evolves out of necessity. The evolution is driven by client and firm pressures, typically based on the profitability (firm) cost center predictability and outcome (client) groups most in need of help.

About the authors

Toby Brown

Toby is the director of strategic pricing & analytics for Akin Gump (www.akingump.com). In this role Toby works with firm partners and clients in developing pricing arrangements and service delivery models that drive successful relationships. Prior to this, Toby served in similar roles for both Vinson & Elkins and Fulbright & Jaworski, where he also drove knowledge management (KM) initiatives and various marketing efforts. Before joining Fulbright, Toby served as the communications director for the Utah State Bar. In his tenure with the Bar, he also served as the CLE, access to justice and programs director.

Toby presents nationally on legal pricing, marketing, technology, and law firm management for associations, law firms, legal departments, law schools, and paralegal programs. He has also published numerous articles on these topics. Toby has served on a number of legal services boards, bar association task forces, and legal market organizations. He received the Peer Excellence Award, the President's Award, and the Anne Charles Award from the National Association of Bar Executives.

Toby maintains the ABA award-winning *3 Geeks and a Law Blog* with two colleagues at: www.geeklawblog.com. He is active on Twitter as @gnawledge and can be found on LinkedIn at www.linkedin.com/in/tobinbrown.

Vincent Cordo

Vince serves as the global director of client value for Reed Smith. He leads the firm strategy related to the evaluation and implementation of value pricing, alternative fee arrangements (AFAs) and matter management. He is responsible for organizing efficient and capable teams of professionals to align project management and process improvement with business drivers, assigning resources, tools, and tactics to satisfy business and client needs.

As the leader of Reed Smith's project management office (PMO), Vince oversees the strategy and application of legal project management, while working to drive efforts to define and deliver maximum value to clients. His team includes financial analysts and project managers who prepare and analyze various pricing alternatives, and who assist with matter management firmwide.

Throughout his career and prior to joining Reed Smith, Vince has held the positions of business development director, business consultant, global director, project manager, and engineer. In these roles, Vince worked with venture capital firms, assisting with multiple public offerings, and he also took the lead on a number of diverse business, information technology, and project management initiatives for a wide range of clients. Vince is a recognized leader and speaker in the fields of AFAs, project management, business process improvement, knowledge management, service delivery, and a variety of related disciplines. He is a Six Sigma Black Belt, is a member of the Society for Information Management, ILTA, the AFA Forum, Six Sigma and Project Management Institute, and helped form the legal industry Pricing Practice Innovation Project Management Group (P3).

Vince is active on Twitter as @vcordo and can be found on LinkedIn at www.linkedin.com/in/vincentcordo.

Acknowledgements

EVEN A quick skimming of this report will give you an idea of the chaotic and demanding nature of the pricing role. This of course impacts those nearest to us, both personally and professionally, and taking the time to write this report has only increased this.

First, we would both like to thank our spouses (Janet and Deanna), and our families for their patience and understanding. The interruptions they endure at all hours of the night and day, including during vacations, are far too numerous. Without their support, our jobs would quickly become unendurable.

We would like to thank those who work for and with us. Our teams put up with the same intensity and demands as us, but they also put up with us when we rant in frustration. We also make demands on others in our firm, especially those in the finance department, so thank you to all of them for their understanding and help with the constant stream of crazy ideas and projects we continually hit them with.

Thanks to Helen Roche and the Ark Group without whom this report would never find its way to the industry.

Special thanks are also due to our peers in other firms. This growing network of legal pricing professionals allows us to expand our skills and the value we bring our firms. Being able to bounce ideas off each other and share frustrations and small victories makes our jobs much more fulfilling. Finally, thank you to our firms for putting us in these roles and for supporting us in the great endeavor to adapt to this dynamic, ever changing market we now live in.

Chapter 1: Why a pricing role?

MUCH HAS been written about the changing market for legal services. The thrust of this dialog deals with a basic, structural change in the market. In the past, prior to the mid 2000 recession, demand for legal services grew and firms were able to consistently raise billing rates. This led to a great run of growing profitability. However, the perfect storm then hit lawyers. The recession was only the final, yet quite large, straw. Prior to this, as the market became over-saturated with supply (lawyers), clients had already begun pushing for greater discounts. Adding fuel to the fire was the technology revolution which altered expectations for everything to become better, faster, and cheaper, almost daily.

What these forces meant for law firms was that their pricing strategies would need to change – dramatically. Prior to 2007, most firms would raise rates each year in the range of 6 to 10 per cent. In recent years, firms have been doing well with 3.5 per cent increases. However, even with those price increases, a firm's actual realization of price increases can be flat or negative, since realization against these rates has dropped from 95 per cent to about 85 per cent in the same period. Finally, with utilization of lawyers dropping, the cost per hour to deliver services is rising. These factors put firms in a tough position. They either need to adapt and embrace new pricing approaches, or sit back and watch their bottom lines drop.

These challenging times have led many law firms to create pricing roles. Given the pressures on partners to bring in business, these roles quickly became important within firms and have high value to firm leadership. The titles for these positions can vary, but generally they evolve into some form of a 'pricing director'. The director level acknowledges the impact on the business of law and the need for high-level skills for the position.

Pricing directors (and their equivalents) have been thrust into the position of helping their firms to understand and ultimately to adapt to this changing legal market. To function in this role, one needs a breadth of skills which include: financial, practice management, technology, marketing, business development, and knowledge management. Another challenge for the role is its unique nature. It does not necessarily fit neatly into one existing department within a law firm. Some pricing directors serve in the finance department, while others serve in marketing, knowledge management, or even general administration. Needless to say, whatever the role starts as, and whichever department it starts in, it invariably evolves out of necessity. The evolution is driven by internal firm pressures, typically based on the practice groups most in need of help. Plus, it is driven by external forces, typically the types of clients exerting the greatest pricing pressures. For simplicity, the majority of this report will refer to the specific title of 'pricing director' but law firms and readers can assume the theory can be applied to the variations on this title. The report will also refer to a 'pricing team', and the final chapter will provide detailed advice on building this team.

From a high level, pricing roles cover the following ground:

- Interacting directly with clients to determine fee goals;
- Interacting with law firm partners to set strategy;
- Proposing pricing structures that align client and firm needs;
- Modeling fee arrangements for profitability; and
- Monitoring fee arrangements once the work has been secured.

Some pricing roles cover this entire spectrum (and more), while others focus on specific components. Whatever the range of duties involved, pricing roles are focused on helping law firms to adapt to change and to maintain a healthy bottom line through market transition.

With this broad range of possible functions, firms pursuing such a role should think beyond the numbers. A seemingly safe first step to establish this role is as some type of analyst function within the finance department. Although the financial analysis aspect is a key one, it can serve as an anchor, holding the position in a back office role. Here the role has value for a firm, but that value is quite limited. It is recommended that whatever mix of responsibilities this role takes on at a firm; it should always be client-facing. Without this aspect, the role will operate in a vacuum, merely responding to basic requests, and unable to give the right kind of feedback and counsel that partners will need. The role really needs to have an eye on the market and on the factors driving client fee concerns. By reading through this report it will become very apparent that the key to successful pricing hinges on an understanding of the clients' motivations and ultimate goals.

This report is intended to help both the firms who are embracing a pricing role and the people who take on this challenge. The report will go into detail as to the functions, the approaches, the challenges, and the skills needed to survive and thrive in such a pricing role. The authors give many examples and share their experiences from years in similar roles. The report provides ideas for best practices and will point out pitfalls to avoid.

From the authors' experiences, the pricing director role has been very challenging, but quite rewarding. It exists at the vanguard of change for an industry in desperate need of it. Finally, as will be seen from the experiences in this report, individuals are still learning and growing in these roles. The last word on legal pricing is that is a roller coaster ride and nobody is sure yet exactly how it will end. As they like to say at the amusements parks: 'Keep your arms and legs inside the car at all times' – and have fun.

Chapter 2: The roles and responsibilities of the pricing director

AS PREVIOUSLY noted, pricing roles can cover a broad spectrum of responsibilities. In this chapter we will explore in greater detail each aspect of what a pricing role may cover. This will help set the stage for further exploration of the role, and will also serve in sharing an idea of the skills and background needed to take on such a role. A major challenge for law firms filling this role is that the skill set is not commonly found. On one level, the skill set is quite general and covers many job functions. On another level, the roles are very demanding in terms of being responsive and in being put in the 'hot seat' constantly. Imagine facing off with the best lawyers in the world every day who need help but who do not hesitate to question every concept and number presented to them. As a result, in addition to functional skills, these roles demand a high level of professionalism and a thick skin.

To cover the skill set, this chapter will take a step-by-step look at what the pricing role might face each time a fee arrangement is explored. This approach will not only highlight the skills needed, but it will give firms an idea of the possible functions the role might serve.

The fee conversation role

Most typically, the pricing role is engaged once a lawyer is asked to respond to a client request. These requests can range from a simple request for a discount to a formal RFP. Most of these requests are of a defensive nature; meaning the client initiated the conversation, versus the lawyer proactively taking an idea to the client. In the initial response, the pricing role should be delving into the core goals behind the request.

This effort starts by questioning the lawyer to get a sense of:

1. The relationship with the client;
2. The client's history on rates, discounts, and fee concerns; and
3. Any specific needs expressed by the client on this matter or generally on its legal work.

The core goal here is an understanding of the client's motivations behind their pricing request. Making assumptions about what these goals are can result in misaligned fee options. So, it is therefore very important to take the time to develop this understanding. These conversations are also important as they set the stage for a culture of conversation going forward. Rarely is one conversation about fees sufficient to ensure success.

If it becomes apparent that the lawyer involved is not sufficiently aware of the client's motivations, then a conversation with the client is the next step. In best practice, this conversation will include the pricing role. In some circumstances, having the lawyer engage with the client on this subject is enough. However, including the pricing role brings an objective perspective to the situation and serves as a train-by-example opportunity with the lawyer.

Experience shows that lawyers, for the most part, are not comfortable having these conversations with clients. This is the case since lawyers may feel that negotiating with a client puts them at odds instead of aligned with the client's best interest. More importantly, lawyers are not trained to have these conversations and usually have little to no experience engaging in them. Frankly, these are sales conversations, which can make many people uncomfortable. The desire by lawyers to avoid these conversations is therefore understandable, yet they are very important conversations. Pricing directors can demonstrate significant value in facilitating these conversations.

In this role, the pricing person works to get the client talking openly about their fee concerns. As these types of conversations are likely to be a new occurrence for clients also, this effort can take some time and patience. Often, the client may not have fully explored the core financial issues driving their needs, so the individual in the pricing role needs to be prepared to pursue many lines of questions and to be fluid in their approach.

There is no pre-set list of questions to use in these situations. Instead, one needs to listen to a client explain their situation and then ask probing questions about the nature of the financial pressures they are feeling, and how different approaches might address those needs. One catch-all question that can be used is: 'A year from now, what will fee success look like in this situation?' This can help the client articulate what their real goals are.

At the end of these conversations the firm should have a good idea of the fee pressures involved and the likely fee arrangements for addressing these needs. To illustrate how these conversations flow, a case study example is included below from a real-life client conversation with a law firm.

Case study: The fee conversation in action

In this situation the client was requesting a fixed fee for a complex, multi-year litigation. The lawyer involved requested assistance from the pricing director to explore how a fixed fee might be determined. In conversations with the lawyer, it became apparent that: (a) a fixed fee quote would be difficult to establish; and (b) that fee would need to be very high in order to account for the different paths such a case might take over the course of three or four years. The lawyer was not sure why the client wanted the fixed fee, only that they were adamant about getting one in place. A call was set with the pricing director, the lawyer, and the client.

On the call, the client again expressed their desire for a fixed fee. The line of questioning from the pricing director explored why the client thought this fee arrangement was best suited for the matter. The client described how they use fixed fees for much of their litigation to great success. The pricing director asked them to categorize the types of cases this covered. It ordinarily covered simple labor cases and had never been used for anything lasting longer than about nine months. The pricing director then asked how the fees for cases were internally accounted for. The client said this is why they liked fixed fees – because, internally, they had to report monthly and quarterly to each business unit on expected legal costs. In turn, the business unit leaders depended on those estimates in their profit/loss predictions, which in turn determined their bonuses. So the client's real driver was predictability of fees on a monthly and quarterly basis so that business unit leaders could earn their bonuses. For small matters, fixed fees were ideal for meeting this goal. For large, complex matters, this was not so much the case. As a result, the pricing director suggested either fixed fees per month, quoted at least a quarter ahead of each billing cycle, or hourly rates with hard budgets provided under the same time frame.

The client immediately saw how these approaches would better meet the needs of their business units with the large matter in question, while allowing them to monitor and hold the line on costs over the life of the matter.

The example above demonstrates both the value of these conversations and the need to be flexible with a line of questions. Without this prodding and willingness to ask questions around what appeared to be the direct issue, the client may have ended up with an inappropriate fee arrangement. This also brings home the point that if a firm does not understand its client's fee needs, it will not be able to meet them.

Perhaps the highest value a pricing director brings to a firm centers on these client fee conversations. Yet, in the market currently, relatively few pricing roles are directly involved in client fee conversations. This is likely a reflection of it being an early stage of adoption for this role. For a lawyer or firm to be comfortable putting a pricing director in front of clients, the pricing director will have to have built up a level of credibility and trust with a firm's partners. It is predicted that this function of the pricing role will become more widespread over time. Its involvement in fee conversations can mean the difference between success and not getting the work from clients. Having the role holder involved in conversations encourages clients to speak openly about their fee concerns, and it allows the lawyers involved in the conversations to develop their own fee conversation skills for future discussions.

The budget building role

An all too typical 'magic button' request pricing directors receive is: 'Send me a budget for a [insert type] matter.' Many partners presume that there is some magic button that, once pushed, generates a budget for any given type of matter. As a service to all of those already in pricing roles, let us disabuse this perception. There is no magic button. Yes, the firm has done matters like this in the past. However, finding them is problem number one. Even if the firm has a list of past matters, what will be found is fee amounts all over the board. One analysis of 35 similar matters resulted in fees ranging from $9,000 to $900,000. Now there were very good reasons for why this wide range existed – and those are the reasons why there is no such thing as a 'magic button'.

Most legal work has a range of possibilities for how it should be managed. This means budgets must be built with an understanding of what the range is in a given situation. In project management parlance, this means scope is needed in order to construct a budget. The problem in the legal industry is that it has not utilized 'scope' much in the past. Many times the only 'scoping' information available is a copy of the complaint filed against the client. This is not a reasonable scope for budget building.

Lawyers are hesitant to commit to any budget number out of fear they will be held to it and that they will have guessed wrong about the scope issues. The reality is they still need to build budgets, be it in response to direct client demand or just for internal purposes. The pricing role therefore serves to get them past this fear and provides guidance and eventually tools for building basic budgets. The following sections will discuss different methods of budget building.

Bottom up budgets

The most thorough approach for budget building is laying out the process of the matter, usually into phases, with the various tasks associated with each phase, and then the hours required to perform each task. Then the hours can be multiplied by the respective billing rates to determine the budget. Not many lawyers are willing to do this and, more importantly, at this stage in the evolution of pricing, they probably should not be doing it. The knowledge base on pricing is so limited that they are making very wild guesses about how the matter will progress. Therefore, unless the lawyer has access to that level of knowledge, bottom up budgets will not work well.

Top down

Another approach is starting at the top level of a budget and then working down to an appropriate level of detail. This can start as simple as asking: 'What do you think the fee will be?' This may sound oversimplified, however, a partner with 30 years of practice experience should have a good idea of how much a given matter might cost. Of course, there is a concern that lawyers will underestimate the amount, but such numbers are great starting points for determining a budget.

With the number in hand, the pricing director can test it by questioning the partner. Asking which 10 factors will significantly change the budget will elicit an overwhelming amount of information from the partner. 'There must be 100 things that will blow this budget' is a typical response. When pushed though, there are usually five or six major factors that will impact the budget. They will be centered on logical factors such as opposing counsel, jurisdiction, the opposing party, client business goals, third party intervention, and the like. By isolating any of these that are very likely to occur, the budget can then be adjusted to account for them.

Another way of confirming a budget number is locking down a time frame for the work involved. For a transaction this is easy, since the closing is a logical and often declared deadline in the engagement. For litigation, it can be set around hearings, phases, or even time periods (i.e. through the end of the year). By limiting the amount of time involved for the budget, the firm is limiting the amount of work that can be done – which limits the potential fee.

One more way to test a budget, leveraging a defined time period, is getting the list of timekeepers involved and a prediction of the relative effort each one will provide, multiplied by their respective billing rates. This can be a quick method on its own for building a budget. It has the added benefit of serving as a project management tool, since the partner in charge will know how much effort they allowed for from each lawyer, and can more easily spot those providing excess hours on the matter.

Hybrid

Of course, combinations of any of these approaches can be utilized when building a budget. Whatever the approach, the pricing role can be a key resource for helping partners to develop actionable budgets. In the long run, the pricing role will need to build a knowledge base of budgets such that each time a budget is needed, it can be developed faster and more accurately.

The profit modeling role

Once a budget is developed and the fee arrangement type has been selected, the pricing role can then model the deal for profitability. For this function, there are actually a few technology solutions available. Tools from vendors such as Redwood Analytics, Thomson Engage, Randy Steere LLC, and others can take the metrics provided and calculate a projected profit margin on an engagement. Some firms resort to using spreadsheets as a fall back or even as primary tools for this, but the outcomes should be the same.

Per the counseling role described below, these tools also allow 'what if' scenario modeling. Two or three pricing and staffing options can be compared side-by-side. This effort can help in decision making on the staffing side as well as on the pricing options side. The win-win scenario sought after in such an effort is the right pricing option to meet the client needs, supported by a healthy profit margin for a firm. The scenario modeling is an extremely useful tool for accomplishing that goal. One very useful tool some of these technologies include is a leverage adjustor. This allows one to adjust the leverage at the top-line level to see the impact on the bottom-line. Systems with this tool will evenly redistribute time worked across the proposed staffing model to reflect the new leverage. This produces a more reliable profit margin prediction.

The goal here is providing an understanding of how profitable an engagement will be before a firm decides to pursue it. This is a new function for most firms, giving them much better financial information on which to make pricing and client engagement decisions. Some best practices for delivering the profitability analysis are as follows:

1. Keep it simple (a theme which is stressed throughout this report): Many of the available tools can produce coma-inducing spreadsheets of information about which aspects of a pricing deal are driving profitability. (Note: Profitability is covered in detail in the next chapter.) While useful information for a pricing professional, this is typically overwhelming for the average and even financially astute partner. Instead, provide just the basic information to the approval source, practice group leaders, and partners involved. This might include the fee type, amount of fee, leverage, and predicted profit margin, along with any relevant observations from the pricing director. If any of the individuals involved have questions about the analysis, they are best addressed with follow-up detail.
2. Include comparative analysis: Comparative analysis can come from a number of sources focused on similar work. Similar can mean work for the same client, past work from the requesting partner, or relatively similar deals from other clients and partners. The last option is the hardest to obtain, since most current financial systems do not tag work in a way that makes this feasible. Whichever option is chosen, an identically formatted analysis should be sent to those involved so that leadership and others can see an apples-to-apples comparison. To give an example of when this is useful, consider that a partner has proposed a transaction deal with 7:1 leverage (more details on this in Chapter 3). An analysis of past matters for the client and partner involved can show whether this is a realistic leverage number. If the past work shows 3:1 as the best leverage ever employed, then pointed follow up questions to the requesting partner are in order.

3. Log this analysis: This is obvious, but better stated. You will need a record of the proposal and the analysis. This information will be useful for future engagement monitoring, to track the types of proposals and respective profitability of them and, finally, for use in future proposals and analysis. A significant challenge here is the lack of commercial tools for this logging. This technology challenge will be discussed in greater detail in Chapter 8 of this report.

The counseling role

Not all fee proposals are profitable, or at least profitable within a firm's benchmarks. This is where the counseling function of the pricing role can be of great value. Often, marginal proposals can be made profitable with a few adjustments. For example, small improvements in leverage can make a big difference in margins. Or, adding in some basic scoping language to limit the risks on a fixed fee.

This counseling role is part educational and part coaching. Ironically, lawyers are not usually good negotiators when negotiating on behalf of themselves and their firms. Clients will ask for bigger discounts and lawyers will often readily agree. In the counseling role, the pricing director needs to change the lawyers' thinking about fee conversations. Instead of just saying yes to the client, the conversation role (noted previously) can elicit deeper information from the client on what is driving their fee concerns. This information is key when exploring pricing options. Lawyers benefit from counseling on how to have the conversations with clients, and how to look for alternatives that meet the clients' needs while allowing the firm to maintain a healthy margin.

Counseling and coaching lawyers will help them better understand the drivers of profit, their options for sustaining it, and the types of question they can ask clients to discover the core motivators behind their requests.

Those new to pricing roles can see this counseling effort as 'giving away the farm', since it is teaching the lawyers how to do the pricing director's job. This is not the case. As partners get better at pricing, the pricing director's role will shift from tactics to strategy. This is, in fact, a much more valuable and interesting role to be in. Besides, it is going to take quite a bit of counseling to get a firm's lawyers to a reasonable level of pricing proficiency. Counseling will be a long-term, likely never-ending role for the pricing director.

An example is included below to show where the counseling role can come into play in a real-life law firm scenario.

Example

A client pushing for a deep discount probably has certain internal forces driving that request. Acquiescing to the request may resolve the issue, but this puts the firm in a financially unsustainable situation. Suggesting a few questions the lawyer might pose to the client will reveal that the real pressure is concerns over partner rates. These are the highest rates and those noticed the most by the client's leadership. So, accepting the deeper discount on partner rates, but holding the line on other timekeepers will address the client's concern and allow the firm to more profitably manage the engagement.

The monitoring role

Helping lawyers stay on budget and on track for the fee deals in use is a major function of pricing directors. The basic goal here is keeping engagements on track to deliver the predicted profit determined in the modeling stage. This is such an involved and important topic, it is covered separately in its own chapter later in this report (see Chapter 6).

The approval role

One emerging role for pricing directors is that of approving pricing requests. As the most knowledgeable individuals on the subjects of pricing and profitability, they are probably best suited to evaluate and approve requests.

Currently, pricing approvals are handled in many different ways by law firms. Some firms have specifically created committees for this. Other firms might utilize an existing committee devoted to billing, collections, or rate setting. Some firms get the practice group leadership involved, while others designate the executive director or managing partner as the approval source. Firms with more experienced pricing directors have started including them in the pricing approval role, typically in combination with other firm leaders.

No matter the approval approach, four primary factors should be considered when reviewing and approving pricing requests: finance, business development, experience, and utilization. Depending on the specific client situation, each will have a different weight; however, the financial factor should always be a core consideration. An unspoken consideration for all requests should be the level of trust and the relationship the requesting partner has with the client. The stronger and deeper this relationship is, the more likely the proposed pricing will meet the client's needs and the higher likelihood of success for both the client and firm.

Financial considerations

A core best practice in comparing the financial aspect of a pricing deal – be it hourly, fixed fee, etc. – is knowing what the fee will be at a firm's standard billing rates or, at a minimum, a reasonable estimate of this number. Also needed for this analysis is the proposed staffing, or, in profitability parlance, the expected leverage (non-partner to partner hours). Finally, the probability of financial success should be known, as applicable in success fees, etc. These metrics allow for an up-front profitability analysis of the proposal, showing predicted profit and potential down and up-sides. It is good to know the type of work involved as well, as that may provide insights into the reasonableness and risk of the proposed price and/or fee.

Business development

Some pricing proposals have a strong marketing or business development nature to them. In deals where the proposed financial metrics may not be at a firm's acceptable level, one should weigh the value of the client and the type of work involved. Clients and work that may lead to future profitable engagements will obviously have some value. However, caution is still suggested when business development is proposed as the sole reason for approving a fee arrangement, as lawyers tend to overestimate the future value of work a client might bring. Make sure to put these justifications into proper perspective. One way to weigh this factor is to consider the amount of money at risk and then view that as a business development/marketing investment. If a firm would otherwise commit that much money

Experience

This is sometimes referred to as a 'resume builder' by the lawyers making a request. These engagements might allow a firm to gain practice experience in a strategic practice area or geographic region, or they may allow specific lawyers to gain skills (e.g. young associates gaining first-chair experience). This experience factor can also be used to balance a negative financial situation. It is recommended that these justifications are used sparingly, and only with input from relevant practice group leaders to make sure they fit with the broader goals of each group.

to support a growing client relationship to support a charity or sponsor a conference, then it may be worth approving. (See the 'Experience' example given above.)

Utilization

A final factor to consider is utilization or what may be more commonly called 'productivity'. Practices with under-utilized timekeepers may want to take on financially questionable work in order to keep these lawyers busy. This approach can boost morale in lean times and keep practice skills intact. It also brings in revenue when there would have been none. Similar to the experience factor, firms should use caution when using this factor as an approval justification. Committing lawyers to low profitability projects becomes a problem when better paying work becomes available. Plus, it can set bad habits with partners, as their under-utilized groups will need more deals like this to keep them busy in the future.

The biggest caution – Client expectation setting

When utilizing the non-financial factors to justify approvals of under-paying work, firms should be very careful about how this pricing might impact client expectations. When a client is given lower rates or fees for work, they will expect that same level of pricing on future work and for other practice areas. Consider that deep discounts on high-volume litigation work may sound reasonable, but this tactic may create an expectation for low rates on high-end litigation and transactional work. Firms should keep this expectation setting issue in mind when considering lower rate pricing.

Discounts: Once you cut back, you never get it back

Lawyers who wish to establish client relationships often believe a deep discount is the best method for getting their foot in the door. The belief is that, initially, a client will be impressed with a firm's willingness to give price breaks and will choose the firm to take on an engagement. Now the firm can commit its best lawyers and resources to demonstrate to the client its ability to deliver results and value. This all sounds good until put into a market perspective. In the past, an approach like this may have worked. But it will not work now.

Effectively, what the firm has done in a case like this is communicate to the client that their services are truly valued at the discounted level. And, at that rate level, the client will get the firm's best lawyers and effort. Even with a fantastic result where the client's expectations have been greatly surpassed, the firm has now established a price-to-value expectation with the client. Think about this from your own perspective as a buyer. The only time you think you should pay more for the next purchase, is when the new product or service has had new value added to it.

So, the moral of the story is that once a discount is given to a client, the firm will not get that back. In terms of developing pricing strategies in this situation, there are still ways to impress a client, or show them willingness to take risk without setting their expectation for deep discounts.

One technique for doing this is to disconnect rates from the arrangement. Set a fixed fee for the first phase, or the first matter. The firm can set the amount at a deep discount in order to win the work. The client may find both the fixed fee approach and the number appealing. But, in the process, the firm has not set an expectation that it will deeply discount rates for future work.

One phenomenon in the market in the past few years has been 'suicide pricing'. This is when a firm bids a number at which they cannot be profitable and may in fact be losing money. Based on experience, it seems that this happens most when a firm does not have a pricing director. Partners, with no pricing resource, take whatever action they deem necessary to win the work. For the partner, this is revenue credited to their name, and thus can help in their compensation reviews. It is better to show more money (even with low realization) than less money.

This highlights another key value of having a pricing role in a firm. It acts as a check on partner behavior that would otherwise possibly go unnoticed. A firm should expect its partners to behave in their own best interests, especially when they are not truly aware of the possible negative impacts on the firm.

One last comment here: when bidding on work there is always a fear the firm might not win an engagement. Do not let this fear allow you to undervalue services. If there are a number of law firms bidding on a piece of work, it is likely that one of them will engage in a suicide pricing approach. Pricing wars ultimately drive market prices down, many times to unsustainable levels.

Perhaps the most important consideration in every pricing deal is that of the relationship between the requesting partner and the client. Trust and communication drive a clear understanding of a client's fee sensitivities and pricing needs. In turn, this leads to healthy client fee expectations and deeper, more valuable client relationships. When considering each pricing proposal, it is good to know what level of trust a partner has with the client.

One final note on the role of the pricing director in approvals. Partners often come forward with requests that could be improved. The pricing role can have high value here again, suggesting ideas for improving a proposal such that the client is still happy, but the firm has an improved profit potential. For instance, the pricing director may suggest discounting only the partners in a situation when the client is most concerned with the highest billing rates. The client may have concerns about justifying the highest rates with its leadership and may be fine with such an approach. This allows the firm to maintain a reasonable margin via the standard rates from the associates. This demonstrates a key value the pricing role can have in also making the approval process a chance to improve proposals.

The knowledge role

On the front-end

One of the first projects a pricing director should tackle is developing a process for capturing the pricing requests as they occur. Every pricing request should be noted, logging all of the critical information for each request. This information might include:

1. The partners involved;
2. The client(s) involved;
3. The type of work;
4. The budget (or estimated fee at standard rates);
5. The type of fee arrangement;
6. The proposed fee (if different from the budget);
7. The proposed staffing and leverage; and
8. Any other relevant information (notes).

An approved list of matter types may already exist in a firm. Firms should consider updating that list, taking into account the unique needs of pricing. From experience, these matter type lists were likely developed years ago, will include far too many categories, and can be focused on outdated needs. The pricing role should therefore have heavy involvement in updating this list.

The pricing role should also create a standardized list of fee arrangement types. This effort may sound obvious, but consider that fixed fee, flat fee, and capped fee can mean the same thing for a partner, yet mean far different things for the pricing director.

Unfortunately, not many tools exist for capturing and storing this information. Many firms use spreadsheets or custom database applications for this now. This highlights the need for new technologies to meet pricing role needs, which will be cover later in this report.

On the back-end

As the pricing role evolves, it will need to capture information after the work is completed. This effort will be key in building a better knowledge base of pricing experience and information. Information about performance by type of work and type of fee will have huge value going forward. Seeing how well certain partners perform against budget will be critical knowledge. It will be this type of knowledge that drives firms to embrace structural changes in the way they provide services to clients. It will drive various practice innovations and the use of new methods like legal project management. Without capturing this knowledge, a firm can expect to struggle to improve its pricing efforts.

Again, lack of technology is a challenge but, more importantly, firm leadership will need to commit resources to meeting this challenge, including both personnel resources and technology.

So many roles

In considering the various potential roles of a pricing director, a life cycle emerges. The pricing director has involvement before a pitch is even made, through matter closing, and then feeding back into the next deal. The need for a very broad range of skills to be successful in such a role is also evidenced in this. Those skills will be covered throughout the remainder of this report. Suffice it to say, the pricing role will play a critical role in the success of law firms going forward. Plus, it will be a demanding and interesting role, involved in driving fundamental change for each firm that embraces it.

Lateral evaluation – Future role?

As pricing directors become the profit gurus within firms, a future role for them might be in evaluating lateral partners. Currently firms' financial evaluation of lateral candidates focuses on the book of business the lateral can transition to the new firm. Historically, firms' growth strategies involved a lot of investment in laterals. Unfortunately, the results of those efforts have been mixed. This situation begs for better analysis of lateral candidates before offers are made. Who better than the profit guru to assist?

Chapter 3: Pricing and profitability

PRICING OBVIOUSLY has a role in profitability since successful law firm pricing must be focused on profitability. As noted already, the role centers on profitability: focusing on everything from educating partners about it, to modeling it, to monitoring it in client engagements. This, of course, raises the question of how profit is determined within a law firm. Many times the pricing role becomes very involved in helping shape that definition and potentially even deciding which method is best suited for a firm. The underlying goal of any profit approach is driving the right behaviors from partners and everyone else within the firm. So, to understand the pricing role more completely, we need to understand law firm profitability on a deeper level.

Law firm profitability

What makes law firms profitable? There are four primary profit drivers for law firms. Each driver has a different level of impact on profits, and some drivers are losing influence. Of the four drivers, the first three are coming under significant market pressure, negatively impacting profits. The fourth one shows promise, but a full examination is needed in order to put that promise into action.

What is profitability?

Before diving into the profit drivers, we should briefly tackle the term 'law firm profitability'. What appears to be a simple concept, becomes quite complex. For law firms, the challenge arises since partners serve as both owners and workers. Traditionally their incomes have been treated as purely profits, as manifested by the popular 'profits per partner' (PPP) statistics. In order to tackle the owner/worker problem, law firms have devised a number of methods of defining profit. Each method has its pros and cons, so we will explore each one separately.

Each lawyer in a firm has two basic costs: compensation and overhead. For each of these costs, an annual number is determined. Once you have this cost per year, it is divided by the number of hours billed per year, resulting in a cost per hour rate. Total costs for a given piece of work are then derived by multiplying the hourly cost rate by the number of hours worked.

Compensation cost is the pay the lawyer receives for the year. Overhead is the remaining operational costs for the firm, which is then divided by the number of lawyers to develop an overhead cost per lawyer per year. The result is that each lawyer is apportioned a share of this overhead cost. For many firms there is considerable discussion over how overhead is apportioned. As an example, more expensive locations (for example, New York) may receive higher portions. For this examination, we will ignore how overhead is apportioned and accept that a firm has agreed on a method for equitably spreading overhead costs.

An obvious challenge to this method appears: What about partner compensation?

Is that not profit by definition? Partners are both owners and workers, so there is a challenge in how to treat their compensation. Each profit methodology below takes a different approach to addressing that challenge. The first one, contribution margin, treats partner compensation as a cost. The second one, profits per partner, treats partner compensation as profit. The third, net margin, divides partner compensation in two, with one part being treated as a labor cost and the other as profit contributing to a net margin.

Contribution margin

A classic approach to defining profit as a margin is the contribution margin approach. In this model, all partner compensation is treated as a cost. With this fully loaded cost, the contribution margin is revenue above costs. The thinking behind this approach is that positive contribution margins are viewed as adding to the profit pie. Since the revenue generated by a matter has paid for all costs associated with the hours worked, plus an additional amount, the matter added to the available profit to pay partners.

The problem with this approach comes when partners with very high or very low compensation are involved. You may have a zero contribution margin example involving billable hours from a highly compensated partner and this example actually supports a very high level of partner compensation. Whereas, a matter with a positive contribution margin involving a low compensation partner is supporting a much lower level of partner compensation. The breakdown is a result of the fact that partner compensation does not correlate well with partner billing rates. The value of a partner to clients is reflected in a billing rate, whereas the value of a partner to the firm is a product of their client relationships and book of business. This disconnect between rates and compensation for partners diminishes the utility of the contribution margin model.

Profit per partner

Another profitability method used fully isolates partner compensation on work to calculate a profit per partner (PPP) number. In this model, a PPP calculation for a given piece of work shows whether the matter is driving a firm's PPP up or down. More simply, this model states that if all work at a firm looked like a given example, then the firm's average PPP would be the PPP generated by that example.

A challenge with the PPP model comes from its assumption of a fully productive firm. The PPP numbers are derived using an expected number of average billable hours per year per lawyer. If the actual number varies significantly, which has been happening recently, the model must be reconfigured with the new yearly average. Effectively, this means PPP is a 'pro forma' type of profit. If a firm predicts its average annual billable hours well, the PPP method can be very effective.

Net margin

An emerging profit model actually takes partner compensation and separates it into two components. One component is treated as wage, and the other as profit. There are a number of methods for separating those two segments; either by setting some common standard, or by establishing levels of 'wage' for various levels of partners. The result is a net profit margin number.

A challenge with this model is that the resulting net margin will initially have little meaning to partners, since there is no context for it. Partners may be used to hearing about gross margins, before any partner compensation. So, it will take some time before the net margin numbers have meaning.

The descriptions of the various profit margin approaches were kept brief for this examination. Full articles or a book could be necessary to give this subject worthy treatment. For this discussion, however, having a basic understanding of law firm profit and the basic approaches to deriving some sort of standard metric for a firm will suffice. Whichever method a firm decides to use, its main consideration will be motivating the right behaviors of partners as they price and execute on engagements.

The profit drivers

1 – Rates

Although obvious, the following point needs to be made. Billing rates are the core pricing structure used in the legal industry, and the level of a firm's rates is key in determining its level of profitability. As a rule-of-thumb, a one point increase in rates leads to two points increase in profit. Experience has shown that there might be a range of 1–3 per cent increase in profit for each point of rate change. The range exists since it depends on the specific timekeepers involved and the relationship between the billing rates and the timekeepers' cost rates.

Until 2008, most firms were able to raise rates at around 6–8 per cent per year. With costs rising at about half that rate, it becomes apparent why partner incomes were rising so rapidly. When the recession arrived in 2008 and rate increases dropped to around 3–4 per cent per year, law firms focused on cost cutting to hold the line on profits.

2 – Realization

Realization is the percentage of money collected versus standard billing rate. Once you have a standard rate as a benchmark, there are three basic 'events' that drive down the actual money collected against that rate. Each event gives firms a different signal.

First event: Discounts

Discounts are a market signal that a firm's prices are too high for a piece of work. One might think firms should lower their prices in response to this information; however, that could be a mistake. Sometimes clients shop price by the level of discounts. They are not concerned with the actual price but instead focus on the amount of discount they are extracting. Whether this is rational behavior in an economic sense is not relevant. Firms need to adjust their pricing and pricing strategies in response to the market, but need to do so in smart ways. Discounts as a practice are now very common in the legal market for many types of practices.

Second event: Write-downs

These are reductions from a bill before it goes to the client. This reduction signals to the firm that the billing partner decided certain effort had no value. This becomes important as firms look for ways to lower the cost of delivery of a service. By identifying recurring types of write-downs and eliminating the effort before it is done, a firm will lower the cost of the service.

Third event: Write-offs

These are reductions requested by the client after they have seen the bill. This market signal says the client did not see value in some effort. This may occur because a firm did not communicate the value of the effort properly, or it may just be that work should not have been done. It should be noted that, in some cases, write-offs are just good old fashioned collection problems. For this discussion, that problem will be treated as a cost of doing business.

Adding the three elements described and subtracting them from standard rates gives total realization. The final number is important; but the three components are instructive as to what is driving a level of realization.

A side note here. Since many firms have not been interested in understanding these three events and their attending signals, they are not always tracked well. For instance, sometimes discounts are actually recorded as write-downs when a partner gives a 'discount at time of billing'. Therefore, many firms have suspect data with regards to each realization element. They can know the overall realization, but understanding the components will be difficult.

The impact of realization is much the same as that of rates. A 1 per cent drop in realization will, on average, result in a 2 per cent drop in profitability. At least it does when a firm is relatively close to 100 per cent realization. As that realization number drops, the impact magnifies. This is the case since you are approaching the cost rate levels of the timekeepers. This means a firm is reaching the point where net margin per hour billed goes to zero. At a general level, this point-of-no-return is about 67 per cent. However, it can vary based on the mix of timekeepers involved in a given piece of work. Some timekeepers' cost rates can be 50 per cent of billing rates, whereas others may be closer to 80 per cent.

3 – Productivity (a.k.a. utilization)

Productivity is the number of billed hours per timekeeper per year. Most firms will have a benchmark productivity of 1,800 or 1,900 billable hours per year, driving an expectation of a certain baseline level of productivity. For profitability, this comes in to play on cost rates.

When productivity goes down, cost rates go up. If a lawyer who costs $500,000 per year works 1,900 hours, their cost is $263 per hour. If their productivity drops to 1,700 hours, their cost rate increases to $294 per hour.

The impact of cost rate changes on profit is typically half that of realization. Of course that depends on the differential between the cost rate and the realized rate. The closer they are, the bigger the impact and it becomes just like the point-of-no-return seen in realization.

Caveat: Lawyers tend to manage profit by focusing on costs. This is the least effective way to enhance profitability. Most costs are relatively fixed on an annual basis. Salaries, rent, insurance, and technology are relatively consistent costs year-to-year. Firms wanting to enhance profitability should focus their energies on the revenue side of the equation.

4 – Leverage: The great equalizer

The last driver of profit is leverage. This is the amount of non-partner work versus partner work performed. Or, from another angle, the percentage of partner time worked per matter or per client.

It is possible to take a small detour here to differentiate between profitability on the client and matter level, versus profitability on the practice group or firm level. For example, when looking at the profitability of a matter, productivity should be neutralized. If a firm has under-utilized lawyers, it should not count that factor when evaluating the profits for a matter or a client. Under-utilization or low productivity could be used to show increased cost rates on the client level. The real problem with low productivity, however, is not in how a specific matter is being staffed, but instead this is a firm management problem. Under-utilized lawyers are a symptom of over-capacity (that is, a firm has more lawyers than available work). At the client and matter level, the issue is using the proper level of staffing. If higher cost rates are factored in for under-utilized lawyers, partners are motivated to use busy associates instead of those with capacity. This is not a behavior to encourage.

That tangent was taken for an important reason. Leverage is the highest impact profit driver. Firms looking to enhance their profitability will want to encourage the best use of leverage and not let low productivity encourage counter-productive behavior.

The basic economic concept of leverage is that the more workers work, the more owners (partners) benefit. Workers generate the profits that pay partners. Therefore, the more work is pushed down to them, the better leverage you have and the more profit is generated. For many partners, this argument sounds counter-intuitive. Since partner rates are higher than associates', their time generates more revenue. This is true; however, the profit level associated with this revenue is lower. So, good leverage will lead to lower revenue but result in higher margins.

Of course, further caveats apply. Partner-level work should be done by a partner. The mantra here is to push work down to its lowest cost-appropriate labor source. This sounds obvious and reasonable; however, until recently, firms have profited from pushing work up to the highest rate source, which was a great idea when competition was low, rates were rising, and productivity was high.

Further, and taken to a logical extreme, the argument could be made that partners should do no work to maximize profits. Technically this would be correct. If partners spent all of their time getting business in the door and workers provided all the effort, the firm would maximize profit. However, as mentioned above, partners are also workers. Clients expect the high-expertise of partners on their work and, in fact, make many purchasing decisions with this in mind.

Another point to consider is that partner work also generates revenue. In a situation where 25 per cent of the work is performed by partners, about a third of the revenue comes from their time. The bottom-line is that work should be allocated to the right resources. Firms should make every effort to move work down and ensure the timekeepers involved are constantly improving their skills so they can continually take on higher levels of work.

The impact of leverage on profit is very strong, but it is more challenging to quantify. Unlike the first three profit drivers, leverage is more variable. To demonstrate, consider a matter staffed entirely by partners. By shifting half of the matter hours to associates, the profit on the matter would increase dramatically. Conversely, taking a matter that had only one hour of partner time and shifting half of that (30 minutes) to associates would have little impact. So the impact of changes in leverage will depend on what the original leverage was.

Another challenge in quantifying the impact of leverage is that not all leverage is created equal. As a general rule, the highest profit margin timekeepers in a firm will be in the seventh and eighth year associate range. At this point in a lawyer's career, they will typically have the biggest difference between their compensation level and the billing rate level. In contrast, the lowest margins will likely come for first year associates – again driven by the ratio of cost rate to billing rate levels. This does not mean first year associates should not be used, as they are a firm's future seventh year associates.

Market data shows leverage at larger firms to generally vary between 20 per cent and 40 per cent of partner time. In contrast, a Big Four accounting firm might have 10 per cent partner time. The moral of this story is that law firms have room to improve when it comes to leverage, and doing so can offset the negative impacts of the first three profit drivers.

One final point on leverage. When it goes up, the fee to clients goes down. As work is pushed to lower cost resources, the overall fee for a given piece of work should go down. The word 'should' is used here since this is dependent on the work being performed at competent lawyer levels. If work is pushed down to timekeepers who take too much time to complete the tasks, the reasonable leverage line has been crossed. Staying on the right side of that line essentially means higher profits for firms and lower fees for clients. Truly the win-win result the market is begging for.

But what about costs?

Invariably when discussing the four profit drivers, someone will ask about costs. Costs impact profit. Why are they not part of the formula?

Costs do obviously impact profit, but for this discussion they do not drive profit. Lawyers prefer to focus on costs over revenue when given the opportunity. It is much easier to pick at overhead expenses than it is to focus on the revenue stream. Two thoughts to focus on here are:

1. Revenue has a much greater impact on profit; and
2. You cannot cut your way to growth.

The first point has been the often ignored rule for a long, long time. Go back in time (to about the 1990s) and you will see law firm financial management books make the same argument. The basic argument is that you can only control costs within a narrow range since the firm's major expenses (rent, personnel, insurance, and supplies) cannot be changed that much in the short run. This is true as, over time, these may have a lasting impact if managed well, but the real driver of this year's profit will come from revenue, not cost control. As the classic texts suggested, put in place reasonable cost management practices and spend the rest of the time (say 90 per cent) driving revenue.

The second point seems too obvious to cover, but for the sake of completeness, it is worth pointing out that a firm will not grow a practice by spending less on it. Cost reductions may hold the line on profit in the short run, but without investing in the business, it can surely expect revenue to decline. For example, you can spend an hour trying to save 1 per cent on office supplies, or you can spend the same hour building your relationship with a valued client. Far too often, lawyers will avoid the revenue effort and choose the squeeze on costs as a supposed profit enhancement effort.

Why does this all matter?

Over the past five to 10 years, there has been a significant shift in the economics of the legal market. Previously law firms were able to raise rates to increase profit, typically 8–10 per cent each year, with costs growing at only 4–5 per cent. These rate increases resulted in increased profit. About 10 years ago, however, things began to change. As already mentioned in Chapter 1, the market finally became saturated with a sufficient number of lawyers, so economic forces took over and started to impact prices. At first, firms felt this in realization. Clients began asking for discounts. However, at the same time, firms continued their price increases, so profits were only marginally impacted.

Two other forces came to bear in the market. The first was technology. Accelerated changes in technology enabled new competitors and encroachers. However, this change has been on a slow burn. The other force was the recession, beginning in 2008. This forced in-house counsel to increase rate pressure on firms. Leadership in client companies no longer accepted 'no' as an answer from the General Counsel (GC) when asked to lower legal costs. Previously the GCs would say they could not predict litigation or deals and therefore could not control costs. The CEOs, however, had finally had enough. The amount of legal work was not the question. The cost of it was. Clients therefore turned up the pressure on firms on price, to the point of demanding rate freezes. The days of significant rate increases and high realization were over.

Firm were pushed from a 'cost-plus' business model, where profit was built in to the price (hourly rates), to this profit margin model. Now the game is managing costs of delivery such that a reasonable margin is made.

If the four drivers of profit are considered, the first three are clearly under intense pressure from market forces. Rate increases are limited. Realization has been dropping and continues to fall. Finally, with over-capacity in the lawyer ranks at most firms, productivity is dropping as well as driving up cost rates. This leaves firms with leverage as the only real alternative for counter-acting the other market forces.

In this new economic world there is a significant challenge in the fact that many firms have not recognized the change. The vast majority of partners and law firm leaders still focus on hours billed and realization to maintain profitability. Most firms did implement efforts to try to control costs. However, these controls were not focused on lowering the cost of delivery, but were instead simple administrative overhead cost reductions. These overhead reductions have helped stem the tide, and allowed holding ground on profits. This approach will not sustain, however, as no business can cut its way to growth. Instead, investment in new methods and technologies is needed if firms expect to grow their markets and enhance their profitability. To further tie this back in to the overall focus of this report, one other investment is in the pricing director.

Chapter 4: The importance of a pricing strategy

IMAGINE IF there was an easy way for clients to select the best firm for a matter, see an estimated budget with assumptions, and know that the quality based on the budget is best of class. When legal costs are already squeezed and clients are hard to find, adopting a better pricing strategy is essential. Monitoring the arrangement is just as mission critical. Managing the quality and service delivery under these restraints for clients are just as key to staying viable – but it is not the same procurement strategy as pricing technology contracts, signing a new lease, or saving money on printer ink. Raising rates or selecting firms based on lowest price is not always the best answer, especially in a poor economy that is still results driven. From an in-house perspective, getting the best price is important, but defining the impact of profit and spend projections are equally dire. Can a business truly align and partner with its legal providers – can it manage metrics that justify the results while showing future spend?

As profound business people in the industry, lawyers are always striving to find innovative ways to provide value and contain costs for their clients while focusing on what matters to them the most: fostering relationships, producing a high quality service, and reporting on predictability.

The pricing director's team, coupled with the legal project management (LPM) team comprised of dedicated and talented professionals, should emulate the firm's commitment to these principals. This strategy serves as a resource to the teams and clients throughout the duration of each engagement or initiative, and it offers a number of value add services aimed at increasing transparency, cost-effectiveness, and efficiency.

A few focuses on this client value offering are:

1. Pricing: Preparing alternative fee arrangements, engagement letters, budgets, and matter work plans;
2. Matter management and customized client reporting: Setting up e-billing and other systems while configuring matter specific task codes to track work down to phase and task level, customized real time matter management dashboards, extranet site setup, and working with the legal team involved in each matter to increase efficiency and cost-effectiveness; and
3. Value services: Client-focused training and presentations – Secondee pricing/LPM and training clients how to successfully implement LPM and pricing systems/principles and in-house convergence programs.

Pricing strategies for law firms and their clients encompass methods on how to improve profits. How both the law firm and the client can cut costs or sell more, or find more profit with a better pricing and project management strategy is important.

Is there really a disparity between the internal law firm views versus a client perspective, or are they interconnected?

Many clients are bringing in procurement and/or sourcing professionals to help evaluate providers of legal services' 'convergence programs'. Part of this remit is to negotiate attractive rates; however, the selection is also based on key metrics that are important to their business such as diversity, experience, alternative fee arrangement (AFA) menu, and quality, success, and value service offerings. All of these elements play an extremely important part of why and how they select law firms to participate on their panel, and how the client demonstrates cost/quality control to their business leadership, while getting a handle on the legal spend.

One strategy does not fit all, so adopting a pricing strategy is a learning curve when studying the needs and behaviors of law firms and clients. In order to define a strategy that would support either an in-house or law firm specific remit, we really need to take a look at some of the key problems that exist in both sectors.

Key law firm and client needs

There are key metrics for both law firms and clients and it is important to identify these from the start as they will impact on the choice of pricing strategy. The two sections below identify common law firm and client needs/metrics. It is interesting to see where the same metrics exist between the law firm and client, and important to also identify where differences occur.

Law firm

Internal metrics that are part of how the law firm defines 'profitability' are dependent on factors such as:

- Realization/utilization/value to time worked (as already discussed in detail in Chapter 3);
- Profit per partner (PPP);
- Maintaining the client base and volume of work;
- Governing the pitch and proposal process;
- Crisp financial reports that do not require an interpreter;
- Adequate dash boarding;
- Cross-selling other practice areas to existing clients that leverage the firm for only a few practices;
- Legal project management;
- Value services;
- Alternative fee arrangements (AFAs);
- How to manage missing time reporting and ensure accurate time entry;
- The best way to track opportunities (sales pipeline);
- Secondee ROI tracking and contingency ROI tracking;
- Portfolio management;
- How to improve the intake process to avoid billing miscommunications to align to the discount schedules;
- E-billing setup with custom task codes;
- Task-based billing;
- Matter profiling;
- Sample budgets based on similar work priced before (as a starting point);
- How to report on budget outliers to better plan for the future; and
- Dashboards and reporting on budget to burn – Communications.

Client

Factors that are part of how clients can help manage their costs and impact business 'profitability' are:

- Savings to help the business maintain profitability;

- Calculating legal spend and whether or not it includes budgets from 'all cost centers';
- Procurement tools that work best for the business;
- Matter profiling;
- Client value services that can be obtained;
- Ensuring the budget and work are managed like a portfolio;
- Truly partnering with the legal provider;
- The pitch and proposal process;
- How to obtain consistent financial reports/dashboards from all providers that look the same, in a crisp and clean fashion;
- How volume discounts are managed (and whether or not the client is leveraging its firms properly to maximize these additional discounts);
- Efficiently tracking all of the work provided by law firms;
- Secondee ROI tracking and contingency ROI tracking;
- Management of resources and related capabilities the organization needs or potentially needs in the attainment of its strategic objectives;
- How to improve the billing process to offer better metrics on projected spend;
- What AFAs work best for the organization;
- When hiring a firm, how to identify metrics such as experience, diversity, local presence, best rate, quality, and efficiency of tasks; and
- The client's own task codes that make sense to their business so they can better track metrics that connect to the business.

Defining quality

It would be difficult to find a realistic definition of quality that did not have implied focus on building and sustaining business relationships. Quality is the ongoing process of building and sustaining client and law firm relationships by assessing, anticipating, and fulfilling stated and implied needs. The following are just a few quality points that both sides will focus on:

- Client value services: Building and sustaining relationships;
- Value pricing;
- Legal project management: Executing on time, every time, coupled with reporting;
- Striving for positive results and conformance to the engagement (or their modern counterpart, six sigma);
- Structuring engagements that bear on the ability to satisfy stated and implied client needs; and
- Service delivery: The focus on continuous improvement.

Law firms and their clients both recognize the importance of metrics; however, the difficulty lies in getting this integrated and adopted. The ultimate goal is obviously to focus on tackling the spend/profitability/value equation, managing/monitoring portfolios and scheduled spend, while taking advantage of tacit knowledge, improving the bottom line, and proving it with reporting on metrics. How then does one measure quality, and is it measured in the same way on either side?

The problem with metrics is the choice between which metrics are in fact needed, how they are captured, reported on, and checked for efficiencies. For clients the focus is on picking the best law firm that can show facts on how their experience, coupled with price and proper matter management, get the best result and price. From a law firm perspective, how do they deliver the above while ensuring profits and volume is maintained? To form a pricing strategy that makes an impact on the organization, defining the metrics are essential, while producing 'key' reporting elements to the business. Hence the need for the pricing director.

Important points to remember

Beware of the ever-present 'scope creep' problem within engagements. Many lawyers and clients today realize this is an issue and want to track it in order to proper manage future budget and matters – 'scope creep' is more commonly called an 'outlier' in LPM. It is important to assess project management and the tools and systems in place in order to manage transparency with billing, expenses, invoices and, most importantly, changes to the agreement. This is done to specifically avoid those uncomfortable discussions about altering the budget of a specific project. Another interesting thing for a law firm to remember is when they are dealing with clients that are publicly measured on their legal budget metrics. Even with adequate tracking of any 'outliers', the firm needs to understand that this is bigger than the matter. Clients' spend can affect their stock ticker in some cases. Really showing 'skin in the game' is to track and report these 'outliers' accordingly, and partner with clients to see how the firm can help them with how they are measured as a business. A firm should be creative with budgets and future volumes, tying into a long term business relationship and strategy, and thereby showing commitment to the relationship, while building trust.

Some applications and external systems come with templates. However, aside from these tools being expensive, outside systems do not contain the firm's knowledge management of how it would staff, track tasks, and manage a matter, let alone factor in the training of future talent in the firm. Write-offs and write-downs are often a direct result of poor matter and budget management, and this can be avoided with the proper use of the firm's tools and systems.

Avoid making the mistake of only tracking AFAs within the firm. Tracking tasks on an array of matters is extremely valuable, even ones not driven by AFAs. Tracking matters that are aligned with the firm's strategic direction is essential in order to get better at analyzing how the firm prices, manages, and reports on matters. Internal operational costs in other locations may be more expensive hourly on an operational side, but the efficiency could outweigh the cost.

What to do if hourly rates are too high

It is not always about the rates, and firms need to stop devaluing legal services by over discounting and taking on loss leaders. Contrary to some experts' beliefs, lawyer talent, firm experience/presence, and knowledge are not as easily a commoditized service as some may have argued years ago. The trends have reversed, and clients have seen that cheaper quotes sometimes have larger overruns due to the lack of experience or capacity of the cheaper solution. Clients are comfortable with spending a little more if it is justified with metrics and if a commitment is made with service level agreements.

It is acceptable to offer free services. Just take some time to audit and assign values to the value-added services the firm provides, and report on them through training, seminars, and project management. It is crucial to know key client contacts. Who are the decision-makers? Is it the General Counsel, the chief executive officer, or perhaps the chief financial officer? Understand who the procurement contacts are and what their priorities are. Each client has different goals. Make sure to listen to them and follow up. It is a mistake not to audit client commitments.

This internal pricing and project management role is now recognized and exists in client organizations also. They should not, therefore, react negatively to an honest discussion on pricing with one of these individuals from the law firm side. Law firms should recognize that an AFA can sometimes be more expensive than hourly billing for a particular matter. If it does not make economic sense for a certain matter, careful assessment of the potential costs and thorough presentation to the client regarding the basis for the firm's projections will protect everyone against unexpected surprises later. If hourly billing is the most suitable method, it is a good idea to present the actual statistics to the client and provide validating facts because real numbers make the most sense to people.

Chapter 5: Developing the right pricing model based on data

Know exactly what clients want

Increased responsiveness to client needs, added value, and aggressive discounts are the industry norm. In any form of service industry there is an array of pricing menu models to offer. Effective and practical pricing aligned with matter management delivers a profitable solution that works for the client and the law firm. A simplified approach that focuses on how to achieve this will result in an adopted program that makes sense to the business while making lives a bit easier.

As noted previously, most firms would traditionally raise rates each year in various ranges. In recent years, firms are doing well with 3.5 per cent increase and, in most cases, lock in rates for two year periods forgoing these increases. This is not really a pricing model that works. Developing proposals that are a good faith effort to partner with a client to craft a unique means of ensuring quality, consistency, and cost predictability to the legal portfolio is crucial; it exhibits the intent to establish a long-term relationship.

Today's purchasers are developing metrics to have a better understanding of procuring legal providers. Having the ability to make well-reasoned decisions and protect the business involves balancing all factors involved in a matter. This means having more information at the firm's disposal to ask better questions and select the best price and quality. Whenever there is a need for ongoing services such as legal work, clients want to ensure to 'lock' the renewal of the prices for these services. The best time to negotiate price is during this time of negotiation.

Pricing efforts always influence the bottom-line for both clients and the law firm. From a client perspective, they have the greatest leverage at the time of contracting – this is the time for them to protect themselves against excessive price increases and to negotiate all of the hidden and future costs. However, from a law firm perspective, this is the time, if necessary, to state the case for budget increases due to outliers and task-based billing reports – based on facts. The 'facts' part of this stage is crucial, as providing all of the relevant information to the client is important and will help if firms need to approach the difficult subject of price increases.

Law firms should consider including a CPI Clause (consumer price index) in the information provided to clients. A CPI is defined as 'a measure that examines the weighted average of prices of a basket of consumer goods and services, such as transportation, food and medical care. The CPI is calculated by taking price changes for each item in the predetermined basket of goods and averaging them; the goods are weighted according to their importance. Changes in CPI are used to assess price changes associated with the cost of living'.[1] It can also sometimes be referred to as 'headline inflation'. The following is an excerpt from a fixed fee that includes a CPI clause:

'Material changes in the scope of work
We must develop the fixed fee and related assumptions based upon the facts and circumstances as they exist presently. Leveraging your legal project management and pricing resources, the law firm would bring these items to the client as soon as possible. In addition, it is possible that the economic market that exists today will change over the course of this X year agreement. In the event that material changes have occurred or the economic market has changed drastically (i.e. an increase or decrease in the CPI Index beyond 3% annually), in the spirit of cooperation, we mutually agree to reopen the discussion on the fixed fee level. This provision provides for flexibility to revisit the fixed fee in good faith to ensure fairness.'

Should firms create their own AFAs?

Law firms are always seeking key differentiators and attempt to create their own variants on AFAs. However, this is not the best way for them to spend their efforts. All firms have preferences based on the types of matters they handle and what they know works best within their organizations, and most clients will also drive the direction that the firm takes in most, if not all, cases. However the main questions that must be asked are: 'What do the firm's existing clients want and what works best for them?' and 'What does this prospective client need and what can win this bid?' In answering these, firms must recognize that there are only so many choices and 'best price' routes available. Firms should incorporate real testimony on examples of what the firm has priced and how it managed matters in the past into their bids. To ensure value to clients, lawyer experience and who can manage a matter well will determine who is best suited for the job.

Many in-house legal service procurement directors say the same thing. Each firm says they offer LPM and value services. However, it is by showing how it has delivered in the past, through testimony and ratings, that a firm can really differentiate itself. A firm can be somewhat creative with pricing in some cases to align with clients' unique needs, however, the delivery and ability to report on the 'real' metrics are the true differentiator.

Clients value the following concepts:

- Transparency;
- Communication (reporting and dashboards);
- Competitive pricing and testimony;
- Predictability/projections;
- Strategy;
- Value services – For example, firms can have a lot of tools and clients appreciate when firms work with them to set up their own systems such as SharePoint or matter profile systems;
- Efficiency – Business process improvement, offering the same services for less money;
- Project (or matter) management; and
- Training – Not just legal training, but business training also (e.g. contracts 'abstract' training for business users or six sigma training).

We know this sounds good. While these concepts are great promotional responses, they are not easy to execute and it takes hard work to implement. Let's take a look at how they are achieved. Alternative fee arrangements, value pricing and, most importantly, proper legal project management (matter management), play major roles in the solution. Law firms are leveraging task-based billing to manage matters using task codes in a task-based billing approach – on both the transactional and litigation front. Many would argue that ABA codes are not transactional friendly. The suggested solution is to create the firm's own codes that make sense to the budget. To do this, it is essential to work with internal teams in IT and billing to reverse map the codes so they do not impact on e-billing.

Thorough examination of metrics such as historical revenues, 'outliers', and costs is required to accurately forecast the fees of future matters. This internal due diligence is continually incorporated into AFA approaches and philosophies and must be appropriately reported on. Legal project managers should continuously examine all aspects of this service delivery (which spans across industry groups, practice groups, and regions) to understand and implement best practices and align them with client needs and goals. The pricing director should spend a lot of time on how they dashboard, report, and communicate these metrics; and not everyone needs to see all of them. They should pay careful attention to the end use of the information they are sharing and consider their needs, interpretation of, and the uses they will make of the data. Why is this important? If all of the metrics are available but they cannot be properly communicated at the right time to the right audience in a real-time and swift fashion, then they are worthless.

Leverage strategic pricing and legal project management processes, together with advanced reporting, dashboarding, an extranet solution, in addition to finance, and time entry tools to accomplish this.

It is one thing to understand pricing options, but another to leverage the appropriate pricing option that fits the needs of both the client and the firm. First, the firm needs to designate a seasoned resource that can and will run the pricing process. As discussed throughout this report, pricing directors are the new resource in the legal market and they work with the lawyers and finance teams, helping to map the appropriate pricing structures. If no such person exists in the firm, then it needs a pricing and LPM specialist. Many variables, as well as knowledge management, must be considered while assessing the type of proposal or opportunity response the firm will choose. Among the factors the firm may need help with are operational costs, utilization, realization and, in some cases, special leadership approvals. Then the firm must consider tracking these factors for future needs; it is a full-time job.

It is essential to take advantage of the resources available to help while building this model. Strategic leadership with this role cannot be taken lightly. It should not be delegated off to someone in marketing for example. Tracking this information is extremely important so that the firm can not only standardize processes but, more importantly, track, report on, and train the lawyers (through testimony) on what works best and why.

This can all go badly if the matter is not properly managed to coincide with the budget. When bidding, lawyers can get their 'opportunity blinders on' and forget about the rest of the pipeline management or future budget impact on business. Therefore, someone is needed to measure progress against what the firm committed to and how the client is communicated to throughout the life cycle of the matter. One of the best ways to track matters is through advanced budgeting coupled with task-based billing and real-time reporting. Leveraging task codes mapped to the tasks within a matter's budget is the only way to track this kind of detail. The benefits are astronomical and, if done correctly, the firm can systematically find out what type of AFA works best, and it can gain more control on what is marked up and down, based on the firm's own experience in handling similar matters. It is not possible to get this kind of information from sending out firmwide emails or using generic templates – or anywhere else for that matter.

It is possible to put this into perspective by referring to an example of taking a current agreement with the client based on dated rates, and showing how to pitch new pricing over a two year term. Listed in the next section is an example of a proposed hourly rate for the two year term.

Context

The current agreement with the client is based on 2013 rates, however, as in real situations, a number of timekeepers have exceptions (promotions, joined the firm post-2012, other anomalies etc.).

Table 1 shows an example of 2013 average rates billed to the client (by sample segments often set out by the client), along with 'fill in the blank' proposed new rates.

Proposed rate assumptions

Table 1 represents an approximate X per cent increase in rates. When a firm is proposing an increase, it may need to note factors to justify the increase, such as:

- Rates were held since year 20##;
- Rates will increase effective from 1/1/NEWYEAR (depending on the time of year the firm is working on this, it should take into consideration that a majority of these requests come into the firm in the fourth quarter and it should factor in its financial impact accordingly by prorating increases);
- A multi-year lock, so realization and profitability will be diluted several per cent each year;
- Aggressive volume discounts can be offered (see further below); or
- Consider negotiating some type of CPI protection clause.

	2013 Rate		**Proposed 2 year rate**		**Realization**
	Rate	*Hours Worked*	*Rate*	*Increase over 2013*	
20–25 years					
10–20 years					
5–10 years					
7+ years					
3–7 years					
0–3 years					
			Average		

Table 1: Sample rate chart

Proposed volume discounts

Context

See Table 2 for recent fee billing and realization history.

Volume discount assumptions – Based on spend

Note that this can also be based on matter count as well as other criteria. Based on recent billing history, the total needs to reflect the firm's actionable/reasonable breakpoint and should include any AFAs in the annual billings figures for volume discount calculations – but AFAs will not be subject to additional spend rebates.

The firm can, and should, be creative here by adding a volume discount chart that maps out the schedule of discounting based on spend. It is also possible to base this on matter count. The point is to be creative and base it on the client's needs.

Would service level models work in legal? There are many approaches in other businesses that are used for expansion. What would the 'pro sales blue chip sales resource do'? Regardless of what model or models are selected that work best for the firm; it needs to track how it affects profitability.

A pricing model based on the firm's tacit data

To develop the right pricing model based on the firm's tacit data is a great place to start. This does not mean, however, that one template will work everywhere.

There always seem to be two types of models within a law firm: one being the firm starting point model; and the other is specific to the client that would need financial impact analysis and firm leadership approval. Pricing directors have been thrust into the position of helping their firms to understand and ultimately adapt to:

- Key business trends affecting associates;
- The firm's individual financial performance;
- Client and matter profitability;
- Client relationship support;
- Alternative fee arrangements and secondments; and

Year	Fees Billed	Billing Realization
2013 (to date)	75,000	60%
2012	85,000	70%
2011	95,000	80%

Table 2: Fee billing and realization history

Rebate across all practice areas		
Annual billings		
From	To	Spend rebate %
$ 00	$ 500,000	0
$ 500,001	$ 700,000	3%
$ 700,001	$ 1,000,000	5%
$ 1,000,001	$ 1,500,000	7%
$ 1,500,001+	$	10%

Table 3: Volume discounts

- Revenue and sales pipeline management is an inevitable future for the directors who understand how to support lawyers in a sales support capacity.

The firm needs to work with a range of clients on the basis of an appropriate fee for the value or satisfaction that is actually delivered to the business from the work the firm is asked to carry out. It is necessary to regularly provide clients with annual fixed and capped fees in many areas in which the scope of the engagement is reasonably predictable, recognizing the objective to contain lawyer fees in connection with all types of matters. This role needs to integrate with the client and legal team to be creative with any opportunity. Lawyers must expect that the director will also support them by building a relationship with the other sides of the business – this is a huge factor in this role.

Listed below are some examples of how a pricing director and their team can do this:

- **Opportunities/RFPs:**
  Assist in responding to RFPs for matters involving discounts, AFAs, and other value-based pricing or for hourly matters that request information on legal project management, value add services, secondee offering, contingency fee, or legal process improvement. The pricing team needs to provide financial data and information, and assist in coordinating with the legal and marketing teams to complete the RFP response.
- **Pricing proposals:**
  Create pricing proposals tailored to meet each client's needs. Pricing proposals can include rate lock for a certain term, or a budget and project plan and other detailed information including competitive rate or task code intelligence, historic pricing analysis for similar matters, profitability, and risk.
- **Intake process, budget, process mapping, and matter work plan development:**
  Owning the intake process profiling the matters appropriately. At the conclusion of the intake process, the team should configure the applications lawyers use to create work product, record time, track expenses, and collaborate. Implement metrics on the finance system and develop an internal budget and process map or work plan identifying firm expenses and staffing requirements for the entirety of the engagement, evaluate options for adjusting the budget to meet a desired price or profitability point, and to accommodate changes in scope.
- **Historic matter information and statistical analysis:**
  Providing historic information and analysis regarding how the firm has priced matters with similar attributes in the past, how those matters were staffed, the realization and profitability for those matters, and the firm can also provide additional qualitative information that may assist with determining the potential risks and rewards of pricing a new matter in a similar approach.
- **Client value and revenue support:**
  Helping lawyers with business activities and processes that help business development and the firm to run effectively, efficiently, and in support of strategies and objectives. Assisting in a client facing sales support fashion. The set of activities include:
  - ☐ Onsite pitch support;
  - ☐ Client or practice strategy: Design, planning, and execution;

- ☐ Measurement of results: Reporting, analytics and revenue pipeline data;
- ☐ Bidding, budget, client volume, portfolio management;
- ☐ Technology and tools, including CRM;
- ☐ Matter profiling;
- ☐ Training and win/loss communication;
- ☐ Practice and industry design and optimization;
- ☐ Relationship management; and
- ☐ Lead generation/procurement programs.

The client value and pricing teams are often the liaisons for procurement to other parts of the law firm such as KM, finance, marketing, and IT. They also represent the needs of the lawyers in meetings and cross-functional projects.

- **Revenue cycle management:**
  Taking steps to ensure that the firm is getting paid for the work executed in a timely fashion. The revenue cycle starts when the engagement begins. This role can help in improving efficiency in collections.
- **Engagement letter/opportunity response pricing language:**
  Every engagement letter or opportunity response should fully delineate the terms of the engagement and include a detailed scope of work and assumptions, as well as an escape clause which explains what happens in the event that the scope of work changes. The pricing and LPM team should assist in drafting detailed pricing engagement letter language in order to increase firm realization and profitability and to reduce fee disputes, write-downs, and write-offs. Further, once the matter is in place, the LPM team will be versed on what to track; helping with more efficient tracking of missing time and management of all other aspects of the engagement.
- **Competitive intelligence:**
  Providing information and analysis on what other firms have charged for comparable work, the level and type of staffing they used, as well as the structure of their fee arrangements is essential. In addition, working with clients' pricing teams to understand what was previously charged for other work and what price is right for them is key.
- **Task code implementation and mapping:**
  After a matter is underway, leveraging the LPM team can help with establishing matter specific task codes to assist with matter management and for the purpose of creating a database of historic pricing information.
- **Reporting and dashboarding**:
  Provide customized matter management dashboards and reports measuring the budget, task, and work plan performance on a real-time basis, and monitor profitability in order to assist the firm's lawyers with matter management, staffing, and to ensure it is handled in the most efficient and cost-effective way possible.
- **Matter management:**
  Have a committed LPM team that is involved in managing matters from start to completion. In addition to assisting with task code implementation and providing matter management reporting, the LPM team should facilitate regular legal team and client portfolio meetings to review financial metrics and progress, discuss potential road blocks and changes in the original assumptions and scope of work, and manage and plan upcoming tasks.
- **Knowledge management:**
  Having a disciplined approach to knowledge management (KM) by making the best use of knowledge. Focusing on

tools and processes such as acquiring, creating, and sharing knowledge and the cultural and technical foundations that support them based on:

- ☐ People – How to increase the ability of the firm to influence clients with their knowledge;
- ☐ Processes – The approach varies from client to client;
- ☐ Technology – It needs to be chosen only after all the requirements of a knowledge management initiative have been established;
- ☐ Culture – The biggest enabler of success; and
- ☐ Structure – The business processes and organizational structures that facilitate knowledge sharing.

- **Education and training:**
  Create and provide firm and client presentations on issues such as maintaining profitability on matters, e-billing setup, matter profiling, metrics, legal project management techniques, and delivering client value and cost-efficiency. In this challenging economic climate, in-house legal counsel face a variety of challenges in managing and controlling workload and legal spend and they are under increasing pressure to improve value and efficiency and improve legal processes. The LPM team could partner with firm lawyers and in-house legal departments to come up with creative ways to increase cost-effectiveness and value and to provide training and consultation to respond to their needs.
- **Technology:**
  Leverage the firm and client tools that can assist with matter/portfolio management. For example, managing matter profiling systems, extranet sites for an individual matter or portfolio of matters. Provide the client with the ability to access real-time matter management financial reporting, the documents associated with a matter or portfolio of matters, and an updated process map or matter work plan that establishes the time frames, tasks, and the status of completion of those tasks and the legal team members responsible. This assists the client in keeping track of how each matter is progressing in relation to the matter work plan and budget.

Reference

1. See: www.investopedia.com/terms/c/consumerpriceindex.asp.

Chapter 6: Engagement monitoring

THE PRICING role assists lawyers in securing work with creative and client driven solutions. However, once these engagements are in place, lawyers have a new challenge – actually providing the services under these new, creative fee arrangements. A core resource for meeting this challenge is engagement monitoring. Most lawyers know they need to manage legal work more efficiently over time, but without actionable information, it is difficult for them to know when and how to make changes to their staffing and practice approaches. This is where monitoring (and the pricing director's responsibilities for this) comes into play.

How to monitor

At its simplest level, monitoring is typically approached as some level of budget-to-performance reporting. It is important to note the use of the term 'simplest', because it is, in fact, not always that simple. However, the idea is to provide lawyers with updates on how they are performing against the deals a firm accepts and the pricing arrangements agreed.

An obvious example is working against a fixed fee. In this scenario, the billing lawyer will receive reports on billings against that fixed fee. These can be regular, monthly reports, or they might be triggered at certain thresholds of a budget (e.g. 50 per cent). These reports are meant to give the lawyer the options to alter how work is being managed or, in the event of scope-creep, to contact the client proactively about adjusting the fee arrangement. Without these types of updates, work continues as usual, and the problems of over-resourcing or out-of-scope efforts are not identified until much later, sometimes even after the engagement has concluded. At that point in time, changing management approaches is not an option, and raising an out-of-scope red flag with the client is a bit more problematic (but not entirely impossible).

These monitoring approaches will need to capture all of the time worked on a matter, including time billed and collected, time billed and not yet collected, and time worked but not yet billed. Many traditional law firm financial systems at law firms report each of these metrics separately. So, one challenge is rolling this information up in to simple, easy-to-understand reports.

Complications for monitoring arise when time is not entered in a timely fashion or when budgets are relatively small; such that the fee for hours worked can quickly surpass the budget before a report can be triggered. Of course, this points to the need for law firms to have more disciplined time entry policies. Experience has shown that there is quite a range of time entry disciplines across firms. Some firms ask for time on a daily basis, while others only force the issue on a monthly basis (when bills are going out for example).

Another complication is that a report can show that 50 per cent of the fee has been exhausted, but traditional time entry data does not give any indication as to how far along the work has actually progressed. So, the lawyer could be at 50 per cent of the budget with only 10 per cent of the work completed.

To get to that level of monitoring information, the law firm will need to implement more formal project management. While this is a topic for another report, we will digress slightly here, since monitoring was traditionally a project management function. In project management, a plan is developed and then monitoring is completed against the plan. This monitoring tracks timing and resources, to make sure tasks are completed on time and they are done so with the planned level of resource. Engagement monitoring may not have the level of detail driven by project management but, effectively, it is trying to accomplish the same end. In addition, engagement monitoring should be constructed with an end-goal of project management in mind.

Engagement monitoring will be something new for lawyers. They are not used to having someone else watching the progress of their work in such a fashion. So, the initial efforts will be setting expectations for future, more involved project management approaches.

This step moves in to some of the complications involved with engagement monitoring. These are the basic performance-to-budget metrics; however, they are other important metrics firms will want to watch.

Recall the four profit drivers. Each of those will need to be part of the monitoring tool-set. Realization, as the more traditional and understood profit metric, will need to be included. For practice group leaders, utilization will also be important. And, perhaps most importantly, leverage will need to be measured. Leverage in this sense could be more properly termed 'staffing', and staffing leads back to project management, further demonstrating the connection.

Adding these metrics in to the monitoring mix complicates it quite a bit. Although these metrics exist, they need to be calculated from other data, and current systems, for the most part, have no way for capturing the baseline numbers which are being measured against.

If only more matters were fixed fees, monitoring could stay focused on budget-to-performance. This top-line monitoring of fees will always be of prime importance, however, other metrics need to come into play for monitoring to remain effective. It is probably easy to guess what those metrics are. Referring back, the four profit drivers are: rates, realization, utilization, and leverage. These will also be core metrics for tracking on the matter, client, and practice level. Plus these four ultimately lead to profit monitoring.

Complications/variations

Beyond the basic metrics, pricing should consider other monitoring variations that impact profit, but which will be harder to extract and compare. These are listed with details below.

Blended rates

In this situation a firm will need to monitor the averaged weight rate for both worked and billed time. Some clients are now evaluating their pricing by watching this metric – using it as a proxy for managing overall fees and efficient use of resources (that is, moving work down to lower cost resources).

Leverage

As a core driver of profitability, leverage on the matter (the ratio of non-partner time to partner time billed) can be a tracked metric. Here challenges arise since most current systems are not structured to report on this. On some matters, this monitoring should even be done on a per phase level, further complicating how leverage is reported.

Realization

This metric will probably lose its importance over time. To date it has been a reasonable proxy for obtaining margins on each timekeeper's hourly billings. However, that assumes some standard level of margin for every timekeeper. As rates become more complicated and sophisticated, realization will become a poorer proxy. For now, however, it still has value. For some engagements, it may be a primary metric for maintaining a healthy bottom line.

Profit margin

This metric presumes a firm has developed a well-defined profit methodology that is understood (see Chapter 3). But even then, these metrics have to be calculated on the fly, via a data warehouse, so they are not resident in a database, and waiting to be accessed. Then a firm should have some sort of benchmark; perhaps firmwide, practice level, and maybe even set for a client and matter. With all of this in place, a firm can then measure against it and report on divergent situations.

Tools and approaches

Tools and approaches for engagement monitoring are starting to appear. What is needed is simple, actionable, real-time access to the financial information. One approach used by a number of firms is the deployment of dashboards (which have already been mentioned in previous chapters). These dashboards present the information in simple formats, often utilizing graphs and charts. One recent entrant to the legal technology market sells a dashboard platform, allowing firms to quickly deploy various versions of dashboards. To give a better idea of what a dashboard might present, an example from this provider, Decision Pace, is provided on the next page (see Figure 1). Further information on dashboards and their use is provided in the next chapter.

Conclusion

All that being said with regards to the challenges of engagement monitoring, experience has shown that even high-level, simple monitoring can have significant value. Lawyers live in a reputation world and monitoring exposes that reputation to risk. Once lawyers realize that others in their firm can see their financial performance on matters, their behavior often changes. In one example, a lawyer was losing money on the first phase of a fixed fee arrangement. Once a monitoring program was put in place, their performance on the second phase dramatically changed – leading to a reasonably profitable result.

Engagement monitoring earned its own chapter based on the level of importance it has within a pricing function. In terms of priorities for a pricing department's efforts, it ranks at number two or three. The first priorities will be engaging with partners to educate them, and then establishing a program for capturing pricing efforts on the front-end. Engagement monitoring is the key for the back-end. Once you have the front-end in place, monitoring will be the tool to begin driving profitable practice behavior.

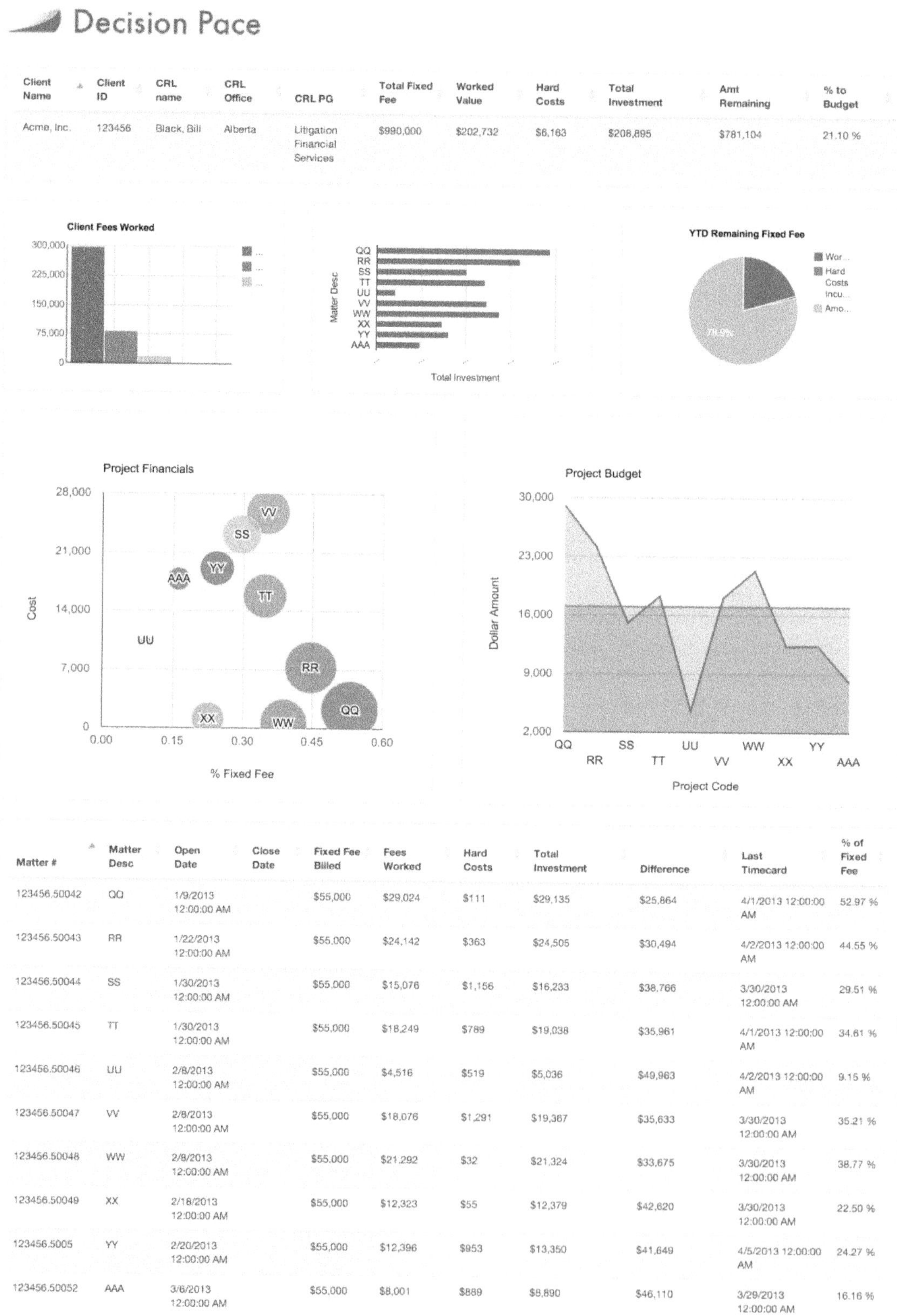

Client Name	Client ID	CRL name	CRL Office	CRL PG	Total Fixed Fee	Worked Value	Hard Costs	Total Investment	Amt Remaining	% to Budget
Acme, Inc.	123456	Black, Bill	Alberta	Litigation Financial Services	$990,000	$202,732	$6,163	$208,895	$781,104	21.10 %

Matter #	Matter Desc	Open Date	Close Date	Fixed Fee Billed	Fees Worked	Hard Costs	Total Investment	Difference	Last Timecard	% of Fixed Fee
123456.50042	QQ	1/9/2013 12:00:00 AM		$55,000	$29,024	$111	$29,135	$25,864	4/1/2013 12:00:00 AM	52.97 %
123456.50043	RR	1/22/2013 12:00:00 AM		$55,000	$24,142	$363	$24,505	$30,494	4/2/2013 12:00:00 AM	44.55 %
123456.50044	SS	1/30/2013 12:00:00 AM		$55,000	$15,076	$1,156	$16,233	$38,766	3/30/2013 12:00:00 AM	29.51 %
123456.50045	TT	1/30/2013 12:00:00 AM		$55,000	$18,249	$789	$19,038	$35,961	4/1/2013 12:00:00 AM	34.61 %
123456.50046	UU	2/8/2013 12:00:00 AM		$55,000	$4,516	$519	$5,036	$49,963	4/2/2013 12:00:00 AM	9.15 %
123456.50047	VV	2/8/2013 12:00:00 AM		$55,000	$18,076	$1,291	$19,367	$35,633	3/30/2013 12:00:00 AM	35.21 %
123456.50048	WW	2/8/2013 12:00:00 AM		$55,000	$21,292	$32	$21,324	$33,675	3/30/2013 12:00:00 AM	38.77 %
123456.50049	XX	2/18/2013 12:00:00 AM		$55,000	$12,323	$55	$12,379	$42,620	3/30/2013 12:00:00 AM	22.50 %
123456.5005	YY	2/20/2013 12:00:00 AM		$55,000	$12,396	$953	$13,350	$41,649	4/5/2013 12:00:00 AM	24.27 %
123456.50052	AAA	3/6/2013 12:00:00 AM		$55,000	$8,001	$889	$8,890	$46,110	3/29/2013 12:00:00 AM	16.16 %

Figure 1: A sample dashboard (reproduced with kind permission from Decision Pace)

Frankly, an argument could easily be made for making monitoring priority number one. Too often lawyers agree to whatever pricing arrangement gets the work in the door, and proceed to manage the matter as they always have. The outcome can be expected: lower profitability due to write-downs and write-offs. This approach also negatively impacts the client relationship, since the client has to spend more time reviewing a bill and looking for write-off opportunities.

An obvious best practice for firms is taking a proactive approach to managing legal work within the budgets, fixed fees, and other pricing arrangements they have. Engagement monitoring will be the vanguard effort for making this happen. Partners cannot be expected to adjust practice management behaviors if they do not have easy (and understandable) access to the right information.

The pricing role is best suited for designing a monitoring approach, in part, since the pricing role can be the driver of monitoring. Some approvals may require monitoring as a condition of approval. Plus, the pricing role is well suited for taking on complexities, and condensing them down to the right level of detail, while remaining actionable information.

Engagement monitoring is therefore key to profitability and a necessary function for a pricing role.

Chapter 7: Delivering the pricing message effectively to the client and within the firm to gain buy-in

IT IS the responsibility of the pricing director to build relationships throughout the firm and with its clients.

It is important to secure the buy-in of lawyers within the firm as well as securing the support of clients, and this is an important step in the adoption of any new pricing process or solution. The pricing director must engage with the lawyers and ensure their understanding and support of any new projects.

An important aspect of this task is proving the real benefit of a process. Two very important aspects of gaining both internal and external buy-in are statistics and testimonials. Statistics and data feature strongly when gaining internal support. Testimonials form an integral part of the buy-in process on the client side, as will be discussed.

This chapter will begin by exploring in more detail how a pricing director can work with a firm's client to deliver the message of effective pricing to match the delivery standards of the firm.

The client focus

Having the wherewithal to visit potential customers, and trying to understand the specific client pain points that the firm could potentially help to solve, is essential. Being proactive means planning in advance. By being proactive, firms are able to foresee a bad situation and take the steps needed to prevent it from happening, rather than waiting to respond to it after it happens. The important message here is to aim for proactive rather than reactive communication. This important step is the 'outreach phase' in which the pricing director (or equivalent) is trying to persuade lawyers, and at some point their clients, that a service and strategy they have designed is going to meet their needs and help to positively impact the budgets.

Some say that first efforts at this will not quite hit the mark and that this is acceptable. This is incorrect. It is not acceptable for the simple fact that, in an era in which people have abundant choice as to who can help with their issues, it is far more beneficial to get the facts in order from the start to align with your outreach. It is essential to obtain initial client traction and then talk to the client base to understand how well the firm's services meet their needs.

Client value

In the pricing director's journey to better understand the legal sales process, some have developed a client development methodology with their management teams. Part of this is a common language to use as new client value is added. Many firms have found that this has helped to ensure client value support is thought of in a uniform way throughout the firm, and that there is a common language to help key stakeholders in deciding where to spend limited resources.

The golden rules in client value for a pricing director are:

- Be available: Make it easy for clients to reach you;
- Find out what clients' problems are using proper questioning techniques (your client needs your help, which gives you the right to ask questions about their problem);
- Explain how your capabilities can solve that problem;
- Be honest on timelines, pricing, and limitations. You will be surprised how often customers will agree to modifications if you are up front at the start;
- Deliver on time: You always have limited resources and you must put them against the highest potential opportunities weighted for probability and deal size;
- If you cannot deliver on time with the quality you promised, make sure clients understand this early on;
- Accept responsibility for failures and do your best to make it up to them;
- Walk away from projects before you begin if they are loss leaders and/or if you cannot do a great job; and
- Under promise, over deliver.

Clients are obviously crucial to the law firm and the pricing director's role, therefore, involves delivering the message of value to them.

Testimony

There is only one true way to deliver the message of value to clients and that is through testimony with examples of how a certain service was delivered in a previous matter. A firm should save all of the witty quotes and theory as these simply will not cut it; people want direct examples of how a firm has solved a client problem. Some key elements on how to deliver the message are explored below.

Opportunities come in all shapes and sizes and if a firm wants to deliver its message to the client, it is important to start off by helping with whatever size need you can. A firm should not expect to start off with the $200 million bid. Working with innovative businesses/clients on small 'on the surface' tasks will bloom into the big ticket items. Collaborating on smaller deals will often lead to direct access to the GC and pricing leads within a client organization – with resulting impact on various sources of revenue.

One of the pricing director's core missions is to help firms to access opportunities that can help their businesses to grow and thrive. Because of this, many vendors are looking into online platforms to manage these opportunities, and have built tools that make it easier for innovative firms/businesses to bid on work, while also making it easier for both sides to identify the bids that offer the best value.

Most requests for proposals contain highly specialized language that only seasoned professionals understand, and those seeking to bid on projects are asked to fulfill a myriad of bureaucratic requirements before even being considered. Working together with clients to remove these obstacles, tools, and processes will continue to open up the bidding process and opportunities to offer services at significantly lower prices. Building on the early successes of programs such as this, it will help get the message out and promote internal buy in.

Aligned purchasing process

Aligned purchasing process is the act of a client tying in their process with a law firm. The responsibility for figuring out how to succeed in this process falls within the remit of the pricing director. An example could be a client who has explained a particular pain point to a firm and who has then agreed with the firm on their pricing solution. However, the client could have more urgent pain points to solve. Or, perhaps the client is dealing with a budget freeze or the key resource who was allocated to lead the project with the firm has just resigned, therefore resulting in delays or termination of the project.

It is the pricing director's job to figure out whether the client not only has a need but also has budget, resources, and an approval process in place to work with the firm. If they do not, then it results in a situation of putting the prospect into a 'business development funnel' so that non-sales resources can focus on staying in touch with the customer through white papers, CLEs, etc., while the firm's lawyers focus on the near-term deals and hitting quarterly targets.

Internal support

When external factors drive adoption of a solution this can be considered an instant market fit – that is, when a solution comes directly from a client need then it is automatically assumed a success. However, a firm cannot always count on this being the case and solutions will not always come directly from a reported client need. Therefore, it is necessary to create a business case/return on investment (ROI) study to ensure internal support for some projects.

If the pricing director can prove to a lawyer that they are losing business or money, they are much more likely to accept a solution to their problems. The secret lies in a straightforward business case for the adoption of a pricing solution. Often other lawyers and clients may think a solution is useful, but just do not have the time, budget, or inclination to adopt it without a compelling event.

The nature of reporting – Statistics

Statistics are an essential element of the pricing role and can be an important feature in gaining buy-in. Pricing and LPM resources need to work throughout an organization helping to solve practical problems. Statistics use reporting and dashboarding to organize and analyze data, and the LPMs command specialized tools. However, the emphasis needs to be maintained on the data being understood and the problem being solved – rather than on reporting it for its own sake.

Understanding the reporting and metrics is crucial. Legal project management and pricing experts must know more than just metrics. These resources need the ability to work with other people, build relationships, to listen, and to communicate. This information must then be used effectively within the firm to educate partners and lawyers on the pricing strategy (as already highlighted as a key responsibility of this role) and the options available, which will help in the achievement of buy-in for new processes or pricing arrangements.

Keeping your message crisp and compelling

The importance of being accurate, crisp, and compelling in communications is without a doubt the single most important aspect of delivering a message. While every effort can be made to match the perspective of messages to the client and lawyers (depending on who the pricing director/team is targeting), and to be completely transparent about what needs to be conveyed, it is still possible to fail to convey the intended message.

Dashboards or 'one pagers' have become a popular means to deliver important information at a glance, as previously discussed in Chapter 6 – but they better incorporate effective visual design. Any one pager that fails to deliver the information that people need clearly and quickly will never be used. Effective dashboards are the product of informed visual design. There are important questions to bear in mind when using these tools:

- What the dashboard is, what it is for, and why it is important;
- The primary goals and challenges of crisp communications; and
- The importance of designing dashboards and communications that are aligned with the way lawyers and clients see and think.

The most effective leaders make a special effort to ensure they provide accurate communication by conveying the intended meaning without misrepresentation or omission.

Delivering the message

Crisp communication means selecting just a few carefully chosen metrics, coupled with attractive and easy-to-follow visuals, and key metrics that both the clients and lawyers want to see.

Compelling communication means being persuasive, holding the attention of the listener, and motivating them to action by use of actual numbers and impact on the bottom line. What is the bottom line? For law firms that could be improving realization on a matter, or enhancing profitability through better pricing and wins by using metrics in RFP responses showing AFA examples and experience. If a pricing director can get their point across to lawyers on just key elements such as the above, they are on their way to success. Although the value of these metrics is obvious to the experienced professional, they each bring their own challenges that make it difficult to be consistent with their application during critically important matters. This is where LPM, once again, ties into the message and how matters are monitored and outliers are communicated.

Delivering the message to clients in particular is really all about showcasing why the firm's quality of services is better, and providing information on diversity and other pricing metrics, volume discounting, and portfolio management. By taking these elements and creating a signature style of communication with the client, both verbal and written, this enables lawyers to have the desired level of impact and influence with their clients. Do not use drone communications in your offering or, even worse, cookie cut the message – anyone can google AFAs and come up with the standard description of them. It is when a firm can combine the message with real examples relevant to the client's need that the message is best accepted both by the lawyers in the firm and the clients.

Communications are less crisp when we attempt to express certain metrics that have not yet been sufficiently thought through, or when we try to convey everything we know about a subject rather than paring it down to its essence. The message is less compelling when you are not sure of your own conviction toward the points being made or when you are not fully aligned with the goals and motivations of lawyers or clients.

In situations in which there is time to carefully craft a message, such as in a written report or a formal presentation, it is important to tie everything into the metrics and KPIs to increase its accuracy, its crispness, and its potential to be compelling. The highest level of client value and sales support skill, however, comes in being able to deliver communications that meet these standards while thinking on our feet, in front of the client/lawyers, in a high-pressure situation.

When reporting is accurate, crisp, and compelling:

- It holds the audience's attention throughout the duration of the communication,
- The recipient 'gets it', and understands how results are achieved; and
- The pricing director (or the firm) are seen as credible, and the message engages the recipient in dialogue and/or action.

When communication is not accurate and crisp:

- The recipient skims or skips over the material, or tunes out of oral communication; and
- The recipient does not 'get it', and the pricing director and/or the firm lose credibility and potentially end up losing the deal.

Successful change practitioners convey their observations, insights, and conclusions to clients in powerful, influential ways. If the client and the lawyer better understand the significance or importance of the metrics and the impact of the budget and quality of the engagement, then they will execute their tasks better. It is equally important for everyone to understand what needs to be communicated and how.

What are the benefits?

In the end it is all about client relationships which impact revenue. Business improves when firms are able to deliver to clients on what is important to them. By initially obtaining internal buy-in, the pricing and LPM teams gain the ability to work more closely with clients to improve the service provided. Suggesting improvements in the client's business processes or systems creates a loyalty among them towards their legal provider. This gives firms the opportunity to obtain feedback, both positive and negative, which in turn will aid in analyzing current strengths and weaknesses, and will improve the firm's future work for them and for other clients.

This all helps in building a strong rapport among the teams with the clients, which is a benefit in solidifying the client's relationship with the firm. In addition to increasing the client loyalty and retention, it also helps in lowering the costs associated with manual or agent-based outreach.

Chapter 8: Pricing technology

MUCH OF what is discussed in this report will benefit from technology. The technology challenge is keenly felt in the monitoring stage already discussed, but it also impacts the entire spectrum of pricing responsibilities. Looking back to the initiation of pricing requests, no tools even exist for submitting, reviewing, and approving requests. Those currently serving in pricing roles have had to do with spreadsheets, custom-developed in-house systems, or highly customized versions of existing tools.

This situation exists since the vast majority of law firm technology was created during the days of rate increases and rising demand. In those days, there was minimal drive for technology innovations. Mostly what was needed was basic data storage and retrieval systems – with the simple abilities to save and then find documents, to capture time entries and generate bills, and to save, share, and leverage contact information. Looking forward, however, it is clear that existing law firm technology is not well suited for the emerging challenges of the pricing role.

Pricing needs financial analysis systems that capture far different information and present it in more simple and actionable ways than currently possible in many firms. One example is that of matter types. Most pricing requests would benefit from access to past matters of a similar nature in order to identify patterns and amounts. On a fundamental level, law firms do not know what they sell. On a high level they know they sell litigation, mergers, SEC filings, etc., but do they know how many of each? Questions emerge such as: How many merger deals has a firm handled? These can only be answered vaguely or with much manual intervention. The reason for this is that firms have never had to ask such questions in quite that way previously. In the past, law firms only needed a few example matters which would enable marketing to show the firm's expertise on a given type of work. Firms did not need to know the fees, the fees per stage, or staffing or location across all of this type of work. This has changed.

The 'expertise' angle highlights the broader technology challenge. Expertise, going forward, will obviously affect marketing, but it will also affect professional development – which ultimately impacts on the firm's pricing. The faster firms advance their expertise on a subject, the more value they can provide to clients, and the better margins they can obtain on their work. This expertise will come through more targeted and directed professional development efforts.

The impact of technology

This may sound way off topic and losing site of the goal. However, what this dialog illustrates is an expanding need and challenge for firms to better capture and leverage their knowledge across all operational segments of a firm. How will they do this? The simple answer is with more advanced technology. However, not just better tools, as, just as importantly, pricing people will need more integrated tools. Another aspect of current legal technology is its siloed nature. The core systems of a law firm – the client database, document database, financial database, and people database – all stand alone. Getting data from one to another is very difficult. Therefore, understanding which clients are buying specific types of services, the staff resources committed to resolving the legal challenges, as well as the profitability of the effort, is a significant challenge.

So what are legal pricing professionals doing to meet this challenge? Beyond making a challenging role even more difficult, this discussion highlights yet another function and skill for the successful pricing director: that of technology expert. This does not mean technology in the classic technology sense. Pricing roles do not need to know how to keep a network running, but they do need to be in tune with the latest legal technology developments and to be aware of how any new tools might be successfully implemented within their own law firm technology ecosystems. The word 'ecosystems' is used since many of these new toolsets are cloud-based and will not need to be installed on law firm servers. They will, however, need to interact with law firm information systems. Cloud-based options will further complicate how firm data lives and interacts in a unified fashion.

This all sounds daunting and, realistically, it is for the pricing role. In addition to dealing with the demanding personalities of law firm partners, they must also have functional knowledge of how a database functions, how it might integrate with existing systems and, ultimately, how it can fuel the firm's pricing knowledge.

Differences in technology and technological advances

Most of the technology discussed so far is classic back office technology. It is the technology a firm uses to run its operations, create its documents, deliver its bills, and collect its money. The 'front office of technology' is about how the firm drives value directly to its clients. The 'Bring Your Own Device' (BYOD) world and the real-time expectations of clients mean that law firms have to have an eye on this world too.

Many firms have extranets they use as client-facing technology. These systems, for the most part, are basic document sharing platforms. They bring value by giving clients broad and, generally, real-time access to the knowledge firms create on the clients' behalf. 'Next generation' technology, in contrast, will have to do more than that. Imagine allowing clients access to systems that generate documents for the clients by leveraging existing law firm content. Imagine clients having real-time access to a document review process. This will be truly disruptive technology; technology that displaces current lawyer functions.

These technological advances and their impacts on law firms have been much discussed in other reports and in the legal press. Exactly why does this front office technology matter for pricing then? The answer lies in lower cost of delivery. What is currently happening in the market for legal services is a shift from a sellers' market to one that is truly competitive. This means providers of services will face ongoing pricing pressures and their response will have to include efforts to lower the cost of service delivery such that their pricing remains competitive and their margins stay healthy. For the pricing role, this means constant vigilance on technology trends and developments. And it means the role benefits from having technology knowledge and skills.

Disruptive technology

There is much discussion on the need for technology that allows 'better, faster, and cheaper' delivery of legal services. However, when it comes to actual examples, there are surprisingly few. There are some noteworthy examples on the retail side of law, where mass-market consumers purchase basic legal services such as wills and simple agreements. Web services such as LegalZoom and Rocket Lawyer are great examples of how the legal market is being disrupted by many new competitors. These services deliver basic legal documents from document generation platforms, allowing consumers to answer a series of questions and generate basic documents to meet their legal needs. These services have generated millions of dollars in revenue so far, which has led to interest from bar associations and solo/small firm legal practitioners. Although these are disrupting the market, the technology involved is not that cutting edge.

A disruptive example

For an example of a more foundational, disruptive legal technology, it is possible to examine a product from KMStandards. This tool performs lawyer tasks on a more fundamental level, since it analyzers legal content and makes decisions about it.

To illustrate the functions of this technology it is possible to start with describing how tasks are currently performed. Often, in transactional work, partners will identify recent examples of existing document types, then have associates cull the deal-specific language to produce a clean draft for the next matter. This is done with lawyer skills and time. The end-goal of this effort is a document based on the most recent law, but utilizing the most standard, non-deal specific language.

KMStandards has a document analysis engine that reviews hundreds or even thousands of document examples and determines the most standard language from the entire document set. Additionally, it can compare a new document against the entire set of documents previously analyzed to highlight missing clauses or highly divergent language. Of course, these are functions which are currently handled by humans.

Technology such as KMStandards has an obvious role in lowering the cost of service delivery and meeting the 'better, faster, and cheaper' challenge. This is exactly the type of technology the pricing role should be seeking out, evaluating, and recommending that a firm should adopt and embrace.

This discussion on technology further demonstrates a couple of issues facing the pricing role. First, the range of skills that will have value for this role are broad. (This will be covered in more detail in Chapter 11.) Second, if firms are going to succeed, they will have to meet the 'better, faster, and cheaper' challenge head on.

Technology caution: Build it and they will not come

The history of law firm technology initiatives is littered with good intentions. Firms have, in general, sought out and installed new technology with the expectation that their lawyers would start using it. This approach has generally not worked however. A classic example is that of CRM (client relationship management). Client relationship management's use in other industries is well-known and, for the most part, successful. The tool is meant to enable the building of deeper and more meaningful client relationships. This would be an obvious goal for a firm. However, when presented with CRM tools, lawyers have not embraced them. The tools were offered as ways for lawyers to save and share their contacts across the firm, enabling firm-level relationships with clients, instead of simple lawyer-to-client ones and most lawyers did not do this. There was no incentive given in most cases and, actually, there is a risk in sharing contact information. It required lawyers to take time out of their busy days and perform tasks they could not bill to clients that would not give them immediate value.

The point here is that simply implementing cutting edge technology will not change lawyer behaviors. Since the adoption of e-mail by lawyers (and everyone else for that matter), firms have been hoping for that next 'killer app' that everyone will embrace because it just makes sense. Firms wanting to drive successful pricing initiatives will keep this challenge front-of-mind. Expectations that new tools for making pricing easier or for lowering the cost of delivery will be automatically embraced are unrealistic. Instead, leadership needs to drive change and then let the technology follow. Firms are better off creating the demand for tools and then providing them, instead of just installing tools and hoping lawyers will use them.

Going back to the example of the KMStandards tool already mentioned above, one law firm saw the value of this tool and moved ahead with implementation. However, time has shown that the technology has not been embraced. On one front, the lawyers involved saw it as a threat to meeting their billable requirements since it obviously reduces the amount of hours needed to create a draft document. (Lawyers are not likely to embrace a technology that will negatively impact their compensation.) On another front, the lawyers involved perceived that establishing a firm standard for a document type (which is what the tool does) would put their reputations on the line as stating the new standard was 'state-of-the-art' and had their endorsement. Fearing criticism from fellow lawyers, those involved were quite hesitant to do this. What this shows is that, without a definite requirement to use it – be it from the firm's leadership or a client – lawyers will be very hesitant to embrace new tools such as this.

As an example of technology more directly involving pricing, a firm might require internal budgets for matters meeting certain criteria. This could include those fee deals needing some level of pricing approval, even if the fee arrangement does not require it. With this process requirement in place, lawyers could start demanding budgeting tools. Buy-in for using a new tool in this scenario will obviously be high.

Saying that technology needs to play a central role in driving a successful pricing program is actually an understatement. The pricing role will play an important part in selecting and driving technology solutions. However, there are pitfalls to avoid such as the old rule of making sure you are focused on solving a problem instead of just presenting a solution. Without a direct problem to solve, firms could end up with technology that does not get used, which could ultimately impact negatively on the success of a pricing program.

This technology discussion highlights numerous core challenges for those in pricing roles and for firms attempting to embrace such efforts. The simple fact is that many of the tools needed to do this job right do not exist yet. However, those in pricing roles should bear in mind that it is their role to know when they are and how the firm may use them.

Chapter 9: Beyond finance

HOW CAN a pricing director (or equivalent) ensure they are invited to assist in all key areas of the business? How can they be ready to take advantage of those moments to deliver facts/testimony on how they can impact the bottom line beyond just pricing decisions? The 'beyond' aspect of this means how they have helped to ensure the client commitment was delivered to the scope of the engagement while ensuring quality and maintaining margins. This is 'beyond' just the legal pricing aspect, and is related more so to the management aspect of a matter.

This report has already discussed the evolution of the pricing role. Some firms have actually given this role the alternative title of 'chief value officer' as the role is already gaining a lot of responsibility in client commitment and on the revenue side of the firm's business. There is a lot of thought that the role will in fact eventually evolve into a 'chief revenue officer' role and that every law firm will absolutely, unequivocally need someone within this type of role.

This is role is very different than the traditional business development and marketing support role in law firms. In most firms, business development and marketing are tasked with practice support, CRM, branding, marketing materials, press, authoring RFP content, and practice support, but very little client management, client pipeline cause/effect, or revenue generation. This is a void in the industry and really is a different job.

The reality is that field execution of client support, coupled with marketing, business development, sales, practice/industry support, leading client vale pricing and LPM is a highly skilled full-time job that should have clear, measurable short-term and long-term objectives.

The chief revenue officer (CRO) is someone who applies expertise in 'revenue generation' and leads the strategy for generating more profitable revenue over the long term. Building the bridge from long-term firm strategy to client execution, ensuring that the entire firm has the direction, information, resources, and support to successfully execute in the industry, leading the execution of that strategy; being the proxy to the chairman.

The firm wins by having both short-term results and a plan to ensure that the law firm dominates the competition, generates profitable revenue, and achieves the firm's long-term strategic goals.

Value

Pricing based on the value of a service is important for the client and the law firm. Data is more than the steps that will be mapped out in a budget. For instance, the cost of getting a result is about the same independent of the legal services, but the prices vary with the perceived value the clients are expected to have.

The perceived value will depend on the alternatives open to the clients. In business these alternatives are using large scale competitors, leveraging an internal team, or going a different route with a small boutique. In order to employ value-based pricing you have to know your customer's business, its business costs, and their perceived alternatives.

Data is a very important aspect of the pricing role. Without the relevant data, a firm will not price effectively. Some firms price and de-value themselves out of the market. On the other hand, other firms and clients leave savings, revenue growth opportunities, and volume on the table. By now most lawyers are aware of what an AFA is. While other industries, such as global management consulting providers, have been working with alternative pricing for many years, the legal industry is only now catching up. To understand the various types of AFAs and which will work well for the firm, there is no reason to reinvent the wheel. The Association of Corporate Counsel (ACC) promotes member experiences with concepts and standards, and has created models to enhance its knowledge base. Common types of AFAs or value-based arrangements, along with examples of when they might be used and descriptions of situations for which those fee structures may be ideally suited, can be found on the ACC website.[1] What are the tactics for pricing, value or alternative fee arrangements, and the ways to track the commitments clients desire that are part of the process?

Beyond the status quo

When pricing any opportunity or supporting an existing engagement that is in need of help, the client and the lawyer move from being happy with the status quo, to recognizing the need to change an existing service, process, or, in some cases, the actual firm. The role of the pricing director and the purpose of their team is to identify possible opportunities, to help lawyers with pipeline development and client pitch support, and to navigate the different client roles, testing different 'sweet spots' between the client's needs and the firm's capabilities. This goes way beyond finance and you need to be able to help the customer build urgency around addressing their needs, to quantify the value that a solution would create, and to overcome barriers to make the change. In particular, that means building trust while coaching the client and the lawyers to understand the budget, and its pricing and discounts, along with the most important aspect of the engagement (which is how it will be monitored) to create a movement for change.

The specific results that you need to help to drive during this stage include:

- **Building a sales pipeline:** This is done through more targeted and strategic activities and a better understanding of how to navigate complex client procurement roles, cross pollination, and gaining access to new opportunities;
- **Legal project management:** Assessing previous engagements on profitability is part of this effort;
- **The intake process and collections;**
- **Client value:** Quality improvement and increasing average account size by building a deep understanding of a client or target's business issues, metrics, and KPIs. This allows lawyers to uncover needs across the wider organization, while allowing benefits to be expressed in the customer's own terms to a range of stakeholders;

- **Further increasing the portfolio/account size:** Achieved by understanding the own firm's capabilities at different levels, and mapping these onto the client's needs in a process of structured creativity; and
- **Improving the win versus loss rate:** Via questioning skills, a clear understanding of decision roles, better leads, a proper experience database, metrics that matter to clients, and the ability to make a quantified case for change that covers the full range of value created for the client.

Knowledge management redefined

Knowledge management will also feature as part of the pricing director's role. As already mentioned in Chapter 2, the pricing director and their team should build a knowledge base of pricing experience and information.

In addition to this, knowledge management can help with the new push for experts with matter management if the pricing director focuses on how to best leverage firm-wide expertise and availability. With proper statistical tracking, matter profiling and analytics, a pricing director can help their firm to effectively staff a matter with more expensive resources by properly justifying the need to the client.

The same applies to internal firm leadership regarding the task turnaround time efficiencies. Having the metrics and quantifiable data that permits 'fair return' is a powerful demonstration in these cases and builds on trust.

The procurement process is most obviously applicable when dealing with a direct customer or client. A repeating 'assessment of alternatives' when pricing opportunities are being promoted, distributed to a panel of firms and prioritized by the client is the normal course of business. There is also a buying cycle going on between the law firm and the client, and a law firm can benefit by coaching and supporting the procurement team to do this more effectively. This role has a great deal of experience working with companies and lawyers in this capacity.

Where does legal project management fit with alternative fee arrangements?

Legal project management has been mentioned many times already in this report as it is closely linked with pricing. Experienced legal project managers are a huge asset to firms and clients, providing assistance at the outset of each matter to create a detailed budget and matter work plan that breaks the legal work to be completed down at the task and timekeeper level. The LPM team then continues to work with the lawyers and staff to ensure they have the tools and support they need to manage each matter as cost-effectively and efficiently as possible. This value-added LPM function is typically provided to the client and is at no additional cost.

However, there is a cost to the firm. Historically, a firm would take 20 per cent of the budgeted time on any type of project and use that as the ground layer for how much project manager time would be needed on a project. We see this same trend with LPM. Proper setup of budget with the pricing team, incorporating it into task-based billing, monitoring the time entries, and reporting on budget to burn and other types of dashboards for the attorneys and clients certainly takes time – while not being cookie cutter for every matter. Although there are good starting points, proper monitoring is essential.

According to the white paper on 'The Value of Project Management' from PMI,[2] disciplined project management starts at the portfolio level, where the strategic vision drives initial investments and where value measures are established. A fully aligned project, program, and portfolio management strategy encompasses the entire organization, dictating project execution at every level and aiming to deliver value at each step along the way.

Project management is, in fact, shorthand for project, program, and portfolio management. And more companies are clearly seeing the payoff from investing time, money, and resources in building organizational project management expertise: lower costs, greater efficiencies, improved customer and stakeholder satisfaction, and greater competitive advantage. The economic downturn only heightened that value. An economist intelligence report showed that 80 per cent of global executives believed that having project management as a core competency helped them remain competitive during the recession.[3] Ninety per cent of global senior executives ranked project management methods as either critical or somewhat important to their ability to deliver successful projects and remain competitive, according to an Economist Intelligence Unit survey.[4]

Where does this all fit in a law firm context? Both firms and clients strongly believe that the key to successful pricing arrangements lies in understanding the client's business and their needs. Each client has unique goals and business objectives and, while one alternative pricing structure may work well for one client, it may not work well for another. For this reason, at the beginning of each engagement, it is important to sit down with the client to have frank and detailed pricing discussions and ask questions about what the client considers a successful outcome, what their priorities are for the matter and, overall, whether the client has specific pricing parameters/concerns and the types of risks that are involved in the project. The answers to these questions and discussions help to build a relationship with clients and help to ensure that each client's goals and business objectives are addressed by the most appropriate alternative or value-based pricing structure.

In short, nothing helps bolster the numbers like project management coupled with good pricing. Project management equals measurable results. Creating the firm's own comprehensive approach, through the implementation and enhancement of legal project management and pricing is essential for meeting clients' challenges. It is through this forward-thinking, yet practical methodology, that a level of efficiency, transparency, consistency, and risk-mitigation found nowhere else in the legal market can be offered.

What does the client want to see?

Corporate counsel have no way of seeing the ongoing activities throughout the billing period in real-time, for all of their firms, in one central location. Corporate law departments, in many cases, use dozens of firms for the various types of issues they deal with regularly, and keeping track of everything by accessing that data through a firm's extranet link is not practical. After all, who wants to deal with dozens of individual extranet systems to compile data that should be readily available on a dime's notice? When corporate counsel need to prepare accrual reports and need all of the unbilled time, does it really make sense that, in this day and age, they are having to manually e-mail and call each of their firms asking them to send the WIP over? Another issue that corporate legal departments are struggling with and have little to no insight into are the types of billing practices being utilized by their outside counsel. Are their firms using what the ABA defines as 'best practices' and entering their time into their timekeeping systems, regularly and contemporaneously with the work being done, or are they waiting until the end of the month and 'cramming' time in? Are they creating hours at month's end that they would not have necessarily billed the client for but feel the need to because they did not manage to bill enough through the course of the month? Industry averages seem to suggest that this is what outside counsel are sometimes doing and corporate counsel feel that they should not have to pay for such delayed time entries – especially given that, the more of a delay there is between work performed and date of time entry, the greater the inaccuracy there is. Lastly, clients often react to bills with 'shock and awe', amazed at the numbers and often insisting upon undeserved discounts when the work was performed per their instructions and should therefore be paid for. What is the solution for this?

Going real time

There is one solution, in particular, that is gaining traction. Viewabill has created a product with a solution to all of the aforementioned issues.[5] Their compelling offering seems to be catching on in the corporate legal world rather quickly. Viewabill allows parties to see hours as they are logged, to control spending as it happens, and to address problems before they arise. A number of large corporate law departments have signed up to use Viewabill since their recent launch. The difference between law firm real-time and this solution is that the time entry is not scrubbed – however it is the definition of client value here that is the main point. Clients want the starting point of a dashboard and can start using one tool to portfolio manage their accounts. It is not perfect yet, but nothing is.

What does this mean for law firms?

The point for law firms is not to miss the boat on systems and solutions that make sense to the client. As already discussed in Chapter 8, it is the role of the pricing director to be aware of technologies that will help the firm or its clients in their matters.

The Viewabill example is a great complement to having a system like Sky Analytics, Serengeti, or CounselLink in place and will ensure that the invoices submitted to the existing e-billing system only contain time entries that were recorded using best practices in billing and not 'crammed' time entries. This greater efficiency in time recording and billing will improve law firm and client relationships and can prevent issues from arising. The pricing director needs to be aware of these programs and open to the opportunities they present the firm.

References

1. See: www.acc.com/valuechallenge/.
2. Available from: www.pmi.org/business-solutions/~/media/PDF/Business-Solutions/Value%20of%20Project%20Management_FINAL.ashx.
3. EMC², 'Global services project managers keep teams, projects on track', 2012. See: www.emc.com/careers/articles/about/2012_gs_pms_121112.htm.
4. Economist Intelligence Unit, 'Closing the gap: The link between project management excellence and long-term success', October 2009.
5. See: www.viewabill.com.

Chapter 10: Pricing – A very challenging role

NOW THAT the various issues surrounding pricing strategy and role responsibilities have been explored in detail, an important question that may be asked next when discussing the pricing role is what it is actually like being in this role. As this is a new role in law firms, there is a romantic perception from many that see it is all fun and accolades; being on the cutting edge, driving cataclysmic changes in the profession. Admittedly, the role does (or should) have direct access to firm leadership which brings it a bit of cache. The partners are constantly in need of pricing assistance, which makes one feel wanted and occasionally appreciated. However, the reality is that pricing people are pulled in many, many directions. Add in the changing nature of the role and it results in one challenging and stressful position. Those currently in this position like to say that their jobs change on a weekly basis. This may, for a time, have been said as a joke; however, it is now a true reflection of the role.

One thing that drives this dynamic nature is the conflicting perspectives of the role, since the role must educate, motivate, and regulate, as discussed in the following sections.

Educate

What is usually the first role of the pricing director chronologically is the necessity to educate partners to a significant degree on pricing and profitability. When this aspect of the role is shared with someone outside the legal industry, the response is almost always one of amazement. People are shocked to learn that the owners of the business do not know about profitability. However, in partners' defense, they have never had to know in the past. They have been working in a market that commanded price increases annually, in the midst of growing demand. These people have done very well without ever having to really understand profitability in detail. In one sense, they had strategic pricing, since they raised prices well above inflation every year. This did, however, give owners a sense of complacency. Since they did not need to know about profit to increase their compensation, they saw no reason to ask or learn more about it.

An argument can be made that the market fundamentals changed while these partners were not looking. As a consequence, they now really need to understand profitability and need to be able to price their products in a profitable fashion. So, as the obvious choice to help partners understand all of this, the pricing director or equivalent gets thrust into this educational role. It makes infinite sense for them to take on this function. It gives the pricing director the opportunity to frame the issues around profitability from the outset; to help lawyers understand the economics in such a way that, as they have to embrace real practice change, they will do so in the most successful ways possible.

There are, of course, many ways to deliver this educational message. The best way is in person. Since the role should be pushing for lawyers to have in-person conversations with clients about fees, the pricing role should lead by example and conduct much of its efforts in person with its internal clients; the partners. Plus, when talking about subjects that have a substantial impact on the compensation of the owners, it is best to be in the same room with them to read their body language and better address their questions and concerns.

Changing the profit conversation

Although partners have not had a clear understanding of profitability in their firms, they have been motivated on two fronts to drive profit: billable hours and revenue. The educate function of the pricing role is key in changing this thinking. Effective education on profit will add in the other two profit drives: realization and leverage. By painting this complete profit picture, the pricing role will shift the conversation from 'hours and revenue' to 'revenue and profit'.

It is important not to underestimate the value of this shift. When partners start to better understand what drives profit, and as a consequence their compensation, their behaviors will begin to change. They will start asking much better questions about fee arrangements. They will start having healthier conversations with clients about fees. Plus, they will bring better focus to delivering their services more efficiently and effectively.

Motivate

Once the partners understand pricing, they then need to make it a regular part of their client interactions. Imagine building a home where the builder gave a quote up-front and then never gave an update on the status of the budget. That is how quite a bit of legal work is performed. As previously noted, lawyers, for the most part, do not like to discuss fees with clients. It feels too much like 'sales' and as if it places them in opposition to their clients. However, for matter engagements to be successful, these conversations must occur.

The pricing role is therefore constantly pushing on this front. It must motivate partners to both understand the pricing of a given deal, and then communicate to clients. This communication cannot be a one-time situation. The conversation needs to be ongoing, and needs to remain as a critical aspect of the client relationship.

Regulate

In the functions of pricing approval and monitoring, the pricing director serves as the regulator. This can happen in two ways, the first being in the approval process and second, in a more involved way, in the engagement monitoring function already discussed. The role, at a high level, should be focused on driving profitable engagements, which means being a check on partners when their behavior runs counter to this goal. Even with the best efforts on modeling and planning up front, the execution of the work is where profit will be actualized. The pricing role therefore serves an oversight function, helping partners to stay on track against the original deals they proposed.

For an analogy lawyers will appreciate, these three roles are the equivalent of serving in the legislative, executive, and judicial branches, all at the same time. Or more precisely, a pricing director has to flip through these roles, sometimes on a minute-by-minute basis. At times, one will obviously have to conflict with something they may have just stated.

The three roles together

So, imagine a role that has to move seamlessly between all three of the above roles and then consider how a firm will measure the performance of someone in a pricing role. Which aspect will carry the most weight? Now it is possible to start to get an idea of what it is like in these roles. From one day to the next it is difficult to know what the job is and how to set priorities on the role holder's efforts.

Add to that difficulty the fact that all three aspects are constantly changing. The education role has to evolve as partners' knowledge grows, along with the need to drive more profitable practice behaviors. Motivation is the proverbial herding of cats; every partner responds to different types of motivation. And the regulate role has to cover every type of fee arrangement possible – or conceivably possible.

This role therefore benefits from an ability to 'think on your feet'. If this is all not difficult enough, the role holder has to perform efficiently for one of the world's brightest and most critical audiences. Effectively, the role has to go toe-to-toe with some of the best lawyers in the world on a daily basis. It has to present novel ideas and then defend them against numerous and constant attacks from highly trained and capable opponents. In short, it is a very challenging role.

The practice knowledge challenge

Despite everything covered already, that is not it yet on the challenges for the pricing role. In most pricing deals account must be taken of the actual practices involved and, many times, the segment or even task level of work being performed. At the highest level, this means knowing the differences between litigation, transactional, and regulatory practices. From there it gets quite complicated and interesting, since the pricing role needs to have a working level of knowledge about many practices. Generally, here are just some examples of the types of practice knowledge a pricing director might need to know:

- The difference between discovery and due diligence as well as the similarities between the two;
- An understanding of the interaction between discovery and motion practice;
- An appreciation of how many document turns might be involved in various types of transactions;
- Knowledge of what 34 Act work involves;
- Knowledge of what a credit facility is;
- An understanding of what a 'Markman hearing' is, and how it fits within a patent litigation matter;
- Knowledge of what 'second review' is in an antitrust matter and that it is the expensive part; and
- Knowledge, in the US, of what CFIUS stands for.[1]

So, if knowledge purely about the job of being a pricing director is not enough, add in the need to understand the working parts of every kind of practice a firm employs. Often, this practice knowledge is the difference between a successful fee arrangement and one that is not. This need for practice knowledge adds another level of complexity and challenge to the role.

So, in a circumstance such as in the example given (see below), the practice knowledge can be the difference between a successful pricing arrangement and lost work.

The gravitas factor

There is one final factor. Implied in all of these challenges is the need for people in this role to have a certain gravitas. They need to be comfortable in their knowledge, have honed presentation skills, along with a professional polish of the highest degree. Law firm partners are not prone to put just anyone in front of their clients. The person must be well-spoken, highly professional, and capable of dealing with high pressure situations. Fee deals can easily run into the millions of dollars. There is, therefore, significant risk and potential reward for the firms utilizing this role. Firms will be wise to fill these roles with people who can interact with partners and clients at that level.

A final challenge to touch on for the pricing role is how its efforts impact on current law firm operations. More often than not, whatever else the pricing role does, it is changing the needs of the firm. This means people serving in more traditional roles are constantly being challenged with new requests, new systems, and new ways of serving their clients. Many of these people have been performing these tasks for long periods of time and are vested in the way things are currently being done. As one might guess, many of these people do not like the encroachment on their jobs and their professional lives. As a result, the pricing role can face internal barriers and outright anger from those most impacted by the changes.

So, it is apparent that this role has many benefits; being connected with firm leadership, leading change, and being a catalyst for helping a firm adapt to a highly competitive and changing market. However, the role also comes with a long list of challenges. As a result, the people who take on this position need to be well-suited for chaos and a constantly changing environment.

Example

To illustrate this practice knowledge in action, consider a situation where a client is requesting a 'busted deal' discount on a transaction. This type of pricing is where a pre-defined percentage of a fee will be forgiven if the deal involved fails. For argument's sake, let's say this is expected to be $200,000 in fees over the life of the matter, and the busted deal discount requested is 30 per cent. On its face, one might think the firm involved is putting $60,000 of the fees at risk. However, a basic understanding of deal work shows that most deals fail during or right after the due diligence phase. This is not to say that the deal will not fail at the end of the matter, just that the probability is very high that any deal failures will occur based on diligence. This is the case since due diligence is the activity that confirms the facts provided by the seller. If any of those facts are found to be untrue or improbable, that is when a deal fails. Assuming half of the fee ($100,000) covers the diligence phase, the firm's fees at high risk are $30,000. Also, diligence will be the best leverage of the work, further mitigating a firm's risk. A firm may not be willing to risk $60,000 with a client, but it is more likely to take a $30,000 risk and would take on such a busted deal arrangement.

A legal pricing community

In 2011, five legal pricing individuals gathered at a legal technology conference in the US. They discussed the need to form a group of some sort, to promote these ideas, and to build a network of like-minded people. By 2013, that group had grown to approximately 300 people. So the interest in legal pricing is significant and growing quickly.

The goals for this group are:

1. Professional development for those in legal pricing (now expanded to legal project management). A challenge for these roles exists in finding opportunities to expand skillsets. The vast majority of programs and conferences offered on these subjects are taught by the people already in the roles and more advanced content was needed;
2. To develop a knowledgebase of ideas and best practices. These could be as simple as job descriptions to setting standards for what to call each type of pricing arrangement; and
3. To drive the development of products and services to meet the ever-changing needs of the role. Most law firm systems were designed to support their more traditional needs. Tools for profit modeling, monitoring, budgeting, and the sort will be of great value to pricing roles.

In early 2013 the group formalized as a sub-group within the Legal Marketing Association. The group is now known as the Client Value Shared Interest Group. In October 2013 the group held its first stand-alone conference. The Conference is called P3, which stands for Pricing, Practice Innovation, and Project Management. The initial goal for P3 was getting at least 100 registrants. More than 200 actually showed up and now the conference will be an annual event.

So, for firms looking to get into strategic legal pricing and those in legal pricing roles, there is now a conference designed to serve these needs. To find out more about the group and the P3 conference, visit the LMA website at www.legalmarketing.org.

Reference

1. CFIUS stands for the Committee on Foreign Investment in the United States. When foreign companies purchase certain types of assets in the US that have a national security aspect, they must be reviewed by this government agency.

Chapter 11: Appointing the pricing director and team

EVER SINCE industry requirements prompted many firms to address pricing and appoint an individual responsible for this function, firms have been grappling with what, exactly, this leader should do, how their team should look and, more importantly, finding the right person for the job.

Creating new roles such as that of a pricing director or director of client value represented a step into the unknown for law firms, and now clients face this same challenge in building the same type of team in-house. Lawyers have traditionally marketed their services, priced their rates, written the terms, and/or have then procured this service. The firms or businesses without a pricing director and team are starting to see client pressures affect their bottom line profits and volume of work more and more. Further, they are now becoming the uncommon setup.

The US legal industry is roughly a $300 billion market. Mix in the global net worth, its closing in near a trillion dollars in worth. What this amount does not include is the under-reported and untapped demand by businesses and law firms for more accessible pricing and budget control help. It also does not include the billions of dollars in write-offs and write-downs. Most of this money is caught up in antiquated and stale processes, poor pricing decisions – even poorer matter management – and mechanisms that represent a significant target for innovation and transformation.

Now take a moment and put a number on how much the industry spends on pricing and LPM support. The numbers are dismal. Most firms are just starting to build a team and only have one to four support people on this effort and have marketing or finance fill in. Putting this into context versus the amount of full time employees that are in BD, marketing, billing, or finance and there is no contest.

According to Pragmatic Marketing's product management survey,[1] technology marketers spend 'nearly half of their time on sales support, a statistic that reflects an alarming state of confusion about the role of marketing' in the tech industry. While this is based on technology, there is a similarity in the legal industry. The functions of sales and marketing are easily distinguished; marketing focuses on a market full of opportunities, while client value supports lawyers with individual pricing and opportunities.

This position and its team needs, and is starting, to be taken very seriously, along with serious investment. This is not an issue that is going away; if anything, law firms will start to see it take on additional responsibilities, morphing into other business areas, and an actual extension to the client relationship.

The legal industry is the only industry that has had marketing and business development but very little pricing and client value (that is, client facing 'sales support' and project management). Sales support is a set of business activities and processes that help a sales organization and, in a law firm context, it will help 'lawyers' run effectively, efficiently, and in support of business strategies and objectives. The advantages of client value teams in a law firm are that:

- Lawyers and their business development/ marketing support team should not have to look for the answers on pricing and the matter management tools provided – they just pick up the phone and call the pricing and client value team;
- The team will help lawyers in understanding the value products and 'what was priced, how we fared, and what metrics were tracked'; and
- They will help to close the business with client facing support.

Lawyers want to find the quickest way to get a deal closed, and most would be happy to have the work done for them. However, one of the reasons that lawyers are so dependent on client value/pricing support people for help with individual profitability improvement projects and pricing deals is that the standard marketing collateral are of little or no help during the engagement cycle. The materials alone simply do not communicate answers to the questions clients ask.

The set of client value activities vary from company to company or firm to firm, but often include:

1. Client strategy: Design, planning, and execution;
2. Measurement of results: Reporting, metrics, analytics and sales pipeline/ trend analysis;
3. Compensation, quotas, and policies;
4. LPM: Legal project management, profitability on matter or group improvements, budget monitoring;
5. Opportunities, pitch, and proposal support: RFPs, pricing, AFAs, scheduled rate increases;
6. Knowledge management: Tacit knowledge, technology tools including CRM and matter profiling;
7. Business process improvement;
8. Training and communication;
9. Cross selling: Lead generation/cross pollination of practice programs; and
10. Client support: Convergence programs, pricing system setup, matter profiling and e-billing support.

The client value team members are often the liaisons for lawyers and other parts of the organization such as finance, marketing, and IT. They will represent the needs of lawyers in meetings and cross-functional projects but, more importantly, they support the lawyers with clients – building relationships with their counterparts in the client organizations.

The governance structure at most firms and businesses is comprised of many people who need a relationship with this role to ensure its success. It starts with proof of impact, and then building trust based on actual delivery, in turn basically making a noticeable return on investment. Pricing is not the only part of this role's responsibility. This role, coupled with building the appropriate team to help deliver its value, plays a substantial position in business or firm strategy – leading the pricing, reporting, and matter management strategy.

Moving forward

Without question, AFAs have changed and will continue to change the legal profession. The industry is witnessing the birth of a new set of roles within law firms where certain individuals are now specifically responsible not only for ascertaining the economic feasibility of fixed-fee and other AFA engagements, but also for managing the teams doing the work under those structures. As director of this role, part of the focus is comprised of pricing and matter management, as well as overseeing internal and external resources, creating cost-efficient strategies, and ensuring matter profitability and client satisfaction.

Alternative fee and value arrangements offer lawyers a competitive advantage that gives them the ability to lead the field through innovation, becoming better businesses in the process, and keeping a happy and strong client base.

What are the key skills required for this role? The short answer is finance, business development, communications, sales support, and technology skills. As a member of the global management team, the director must partner with the leadership in the development and execution of a global strategy which will measurably raise the business/firm in terms of profitability, quality, value and efficiency. What systems should the team become familiar with? Here are some examples:

- Pricing and internal financial systems, for example, Elite, 3E, Adarant, SAP, Oracle, Viewabill, Engage, Redwood, Data Magic, etc.;
- E-billing solutions;
- CRM solutions;
- Matter profiling systems; and
- A SharePoint system for tracking pricing and LPM opportunities.

While the pricing director should focus on pricing and AFAs, that is not enough. They should also tie into LPM as already discussed in previous chapters. Eventually, it will take on an even more business development role.

The world is becoming quantitative. More and more professions, from law firms to the businesses they service, depend on data and numerical reasoning. With the growth in the use of metrics comes a growing demand for the services of individuals who understand how to get the message across (almost like statisticians), who are experts in the following:

- Producing trustworthy reporting and dashboards – real-time data;
- Analyzing data to make its meaning clear on which metrics and KPIs matter, and the need to stand out in strategic dialogue; and
- Drawing practical conclusions and strategic advice based on this information.

The main characteristics

Filling this role requires someone with the ability to operate across many areas in the firm or business. The role has four main characteristics:

- Strategic: This aspect involves guiding and advising leadership on the current and future market for the pricing and management of legal services and changes in the way that legal services are delivered;
- Tactical: The role requires an individual who is an advisor on budgeting and pricing options, executing pricing activities, educating and promoting the use of alternative fee arrangements, and leading the application of project management and process improvement disciplines to the delivery of legal services;
- Leadership: This means building a reputation as a thought-leader and trusted adviser both internally, to

partners and other parts of the leadership, and externally to clients; and
- Management: Part of the role requires managing and mentoring a team of professional pricing, financial analysis, and project management professionals.

The director must be able to manage a large and fast-moving work-load; operating across those dimensions in parallel, exceeding expectations in all, and with a strict focus on profitability and reporting on metrics.

As a senior member the value team, the director should partner with leadership within the firm and the clients in the development and execution of a global strategy which will measurably raise the business in terms of profitability, value, and efficiency.

Other essential skills and functions

In addition to the main characteristics explained above, the following is a summary of the other skills and functions which need to be considered as essential to this role (many of which have been touched upon throughout this report):

- The ability to apply a demonstrated mastery of both the practice and the business of law, and independently identify new areas of opportunity to help solve business challenges (both litigation and transactional);
- The ability to implement pricing, legal project management, and process improvement strategy;
- An understanding of task-based billing, finance systems, time entry solutions, reporting, matter profiling, and e-billing systems;
- Demonstrated experience managing and improving the profitability of AFAs and non-AFAs;
- Extensive expertise in project management and process improvement;
- Being able to improve realization by use of legal project management;
- The ability to manage and lead client value initiatives by building process with other members of the business development, marketing, IT, and finance departments, and assuming quarterly improvement responsibilities conjoined with all department activities, keeping projects, initiatives, and staff on task and on budget;
- Being able to stay current while innovative not only with pricing, project, and process trends, but also being well versed in law firm business trends such as alternative fees, legal project management, and legal process improvement;
- The ability to co-ordinate the use of technology to directly improve efficiency and communicate profitability, realization, and other key performance indicators both internally and externally;
- Excellent reporting skills, including the ability to gather due diligence, perform research and document conclusions, and recommendations;
- Outstanding communications and presentation skills, including the ability to address large groups, including partners and clients;
- Data mapping expertise to improve task based billing efforts;
- The capacity to lead and develop educational sessions, including one-on-one training with key lawyers and relevant programs;
- An understanding of how to create a proper annual budget for this initiative, and manage the budget accordingly throughout the year;
- Participating in pitches with clients (including travel to client locations); and

- The ability to maintain working knowledge of all major legal budgeting, financial modeling, pricing, profitability, and project management applications.

Building the team

Adding members to the pricing and client value team to support this effort is essential. What should this team look like? Here is a list of some support expertise needed:

- Pricing and AFA analysts;
- A pricing reporting/statistician analyst;
- Legal project managers; and
- Client value support.

The pricing and AFA analyst: Responsibilities

The main responsibilities of this role are:

- To maintain a budget database: Providing fee budget templates by area of work to have ready as requests to the department for pricing support. Pricing language for the work type and engagements will be maintained;
- A fee agreement inventory: Analyze significant and/or unique fee agreement requirements, special provisions, and terms and conditions to ensure compliance with AFA policy and procedures;
- RFP responses: Responding to RFPs through databased materials. Maintaining calendar and RFP types;
- The AFA website and maintaining fresh content and sharing best practices/wins identified in the analysis role;
- Coding audits: Fee arrangements continue to be established as hourly when they are AFAs. This makes tracking difficult so audits must be performed; and
- Secondment support: Supporting secondment pricing requests and high level secondment investment analysis.

The pricing reporting/statistician analyst: Responsibilities

The importance of this role can best be explained by alluding to the questions that a client brings up during meetings. Pretend to be one of those clients and take a fresh look at the data or a 'standard' presentation. Now consider:

- Would you read (or listen) to this?
- Is it easy to find the answers to the questions that will help you make a decision?
- Is there something about this offering that is compelling and distinct from the competitors' offerings?
- Finally, do you believe the lawyers' statements are proof-points, well-presented, and convincing?

The fact is that very few opportunity replies actually respond to the real questions that a client wants answered as they move through the various stages of the decision process. This underlines the importance of a pricing reporting/ statistician analyst.

It is important to identify the need for client persona profiles. If you do not know the pricing people you want to influence that support the general counsel, you are not communicating. That is why the best pricing people know that the first meeting with the prospect is not the time to talk about their solution or show a presentation. This first meeting is their best – perhaps only – chance to really understand that prospect's most urgent problems.

An experienced pricing person is skilled at asking questions, learning about the prospect's concerns, and uncovering the metrics that the client's management or stakeholders use to measure success.

Reports/metrics/KPIs

- Developing client and firm KPI and ISO standards projects in conjunction with the firm profitability initiative;
- Strategizing on metrics for current reports and new reports;
- Ongoing assessments on live matters and profitability: Work the pricing team on metrics surrounding these matters, including but not limited to matter health checks and end of matter reviews;
- Developing and maintaining systematic methods of handling pricing requests (ad hoc, RFP, etc.) to make the process less labor intensive and more efficient;
- Producing metrics for the monthly report with the LPM team, this includes extraction of data from the system, and contributing new metrics;
- Leading current and future budget tool product development (profitability metrics, etc.);
- Profitability reporting framework: Utilizing new profit capabilities to develop a dashboard;
- Staffing analytics: Advising on staffing strategies in order to increase effectiveness of AFAs in order to maximize successful outcome;
- Financial analysis: Using analysis methods to identify opportunity areas where AFAs need improvements and what is working;
- Financial LPM support: Targeting large AFA programs that need ongoing financial measures/reporting for the success of the fee agreements (in co-ordination with the LPM team);
- Pricing requests: Assisting partners with pricing support (outside of the RFP process); and
- Preparing monthly AFA and LPM summary reports/dashboards and sending these to management and clients.

Legal project manager: Responsibilities

This position provides leadership for legal engagements and will be a key player in driving the growth of the legal project management program. This role will be expected to utilize project management methodologies and tools to facilitate and execute pricing, legal project management, and process improvement initiative efforts across all practices in the firm. It is possible to refer to Reed Smith's definition of the best candidate for this role for further clarification: the best candidate 'will have a keen understanding of the level of legal project management rigor to apply to a given legal matter to ensure best results. The candidate must be able to demonstrate significant intuitive flexibility in the choice and application of various project and legal process management disciplines and tools depending on the type of engagement, and the real and acknowledged needs for matter management of the legal team. The candidate must be able to take a long term view with regard to the successful adoption and acceptance of legal project management and the firm as a whole.' The legal project manager should be comfortable working with and leading teams of partners, associates, and other legal personnel. The essential functions of the role are listed in the next section.

Essential functions

The essential functions of this role can be broken down as follows:

- Assisting legal teams in defining project scope, goals, and deliverables that support the business needs of both the firm and its clients;

- Assisting with the development of large scale budget and matter work plans;
- Estimating the resources and participants needed to achieve project goals and providing input in the budget-creation and matter work plan-creation process;
- Consulting on the use of certain pricing methods and alternative and value-based fee arrangements;
- Defining project success criteria and disseminating them to involved parties throughout the project life cycle;
- Effectively communicating project expectations and status to team members, clients, and other stakeholders;
- Creating and completing 'after action reports' to facilitate the continuous improvement of the execution of the legal project management program;
- Partnering with the firm's leadership, KM, pricing, and training groups to execute strategy and achieve program success; and
- Developing and conducting training on project management, process improvement, and project management-related technologies both at the firm and client level.

Client value: Responsibilities

What makes a great client value resource? In a world in which it is hard to differentiate on the law firm or pricing alone, clients buy from firms who create value for them – through the insights they bring to the table, the solutions they create, and the help they provide around the engagement and client relationship process. Great client value people can be challenging, but they are seen as trusted business advisors.

The core to the client value methodology, client value, has been helping law firms and clients to drive revenue growth for the last several years. It has been continuously improved since its inception, based on the maturity of the positions and experience with leading roles being adopted globally. Client value concentrates on consultative selling – that space where lawyers help their customers understand their issues and opportunities in a new way and then show them solutions and processes which closely match their needs.

Client value has generated vast ROI in identified incremental revenue by focusing on the process the customer goes through, rather than on a legal 'sales process'. Recognizing where the client is in their own process is critical in being able to support and influence them through each stage of the relationship or engagement. There are five major stages in any buying decision:

1. Developing, leading, and coordinating efforts in the pitch and proposal process – between the pricing and LPM groups on RFP responses, proposals, etc.;
2. Maintaining strong working relationships with broader administrative teams, specifically business development and accounting;
3. Advising pricing analysts on group initiatives and projects, i.e. the budget tool;
4. Leading budget template and engagement letter template initiatives. Tasks include working and coordinating with key partners within practice groups to compile templates specific to organization standards; and
5. Attending and contributing to group meetings (providing updates if necessary, developing key relationships with practice group leaders and partners in each group, taking strategic findings from meetings, and working with an LPM

to showcase to the practice group leaders how the client value team can support projects).

Measuring the time spent on monitoring the matter versus pricing support

The final word on law firm pricing strategies and responsibilities will bring us back to the topic of monitoring. The first step toward embracing any change is for lawyers (whether it be in-house or in a firm) to realize that their current actions, however well intended, are not really getting them where they need and want to go. It should be easy to see that the time they devote to a single prospect opportunity (clearly a client value role) steals time that could be used to bill or influence an entire market about the value of their legal services and solutions – this is where marketing and business development should play a bigger role. Someone is needed who shows the firm the way to recognize that client value support is not marketing, and to clearly identify which role this is truly fulfilling.

Think about time spent on a presentation, pricing an opportunity, setting up a demo, or a reference testimony that helped one lawyer work on one deal. Contrast that to the function of marketing, which should be developing programs that influence all buyers in a specific role in one of the firm's targeted markets.

Which job is really pricing and LPM: influencing the attitudes that drive a single client to choose the firm client value (sales support), or influencing the attitudes that drive a market to choose the firm (marketing)? Keep track of the time in each of these categories, for just a week or two, and see where you are investing your time.

Reference

1. See: www.pragmaticmarketing.com/resources/annual-survey.aspx.

www.ingramcontent.com/pod-product-compliance
Ingram Content Group UK Ltd.
Pitfield, Milton Keynes, MK11 3LW, UK
UKHW050231160926
8657IPUK00008B/194

9 781783 580